Real Estate Flipping Riches

The Ultimate No B.S. Kick BUTT Guide to Real Estate Investing For the Average JOE!

By Christopher Seder
Copyright © 2013 by:

Big Sky Property Solutions LLC
P.O. Box 475
Hardin, MT 59034
support@realestatevipcoaching.com

www.RealEstateVipCoaching.com
www.Christopherseder.com
www.RealEstateFlippingRiches.com

If you would like to participate in our affiliate program, go to **http://RealEstateFlippingRiches.com/affiliates** for details. You can also sign up for our mini course and get the rights to give that course away for free.

Legal Disclaimer: *All the information presented herein is based upon the author's research and experience. The author is not responsible for errors or omissions. Laws and legal practices vary from state to state, and from municipality to municipality. Furthermore, laws can, and often do change over time. The author does not vouch for the legality of his opinions, nor is there any intent to supply legal advice. The author strongly encourages the reader to consult with an attorney prior to entering any real estate transaction and contract and before taking any action on the material written or presented by the author.*

The Real Estate Investing Industry Has Changed!

Its never going to be the same!

While some time honored, real estate investing strategies and skills continue to work, it's more important than ever to use new and more sophisticated methods combined with old strategies.

Right now is the Time to get started creating financial freedom for you and your family. RIGHT NOW!

"The single most powerful asset we all have is our mind. If it is trained well, it can create enormous wealth in what seems to be an instant."
— Robert T. Kiyosaki, Rich Dad, Poor Dad

"Every day, you'll have opportunities to take chances and to work outside your safety net. Sure, it's a lot easier to stay in your comfort zone. In my case, business suits and real estate, but sometimes you have to take risks. When the risks pay off, that's when you reap the biggest rewards."
-Donald Trump

Table of Contents

How to Effectively Use this Book

Congratulations! You have put yourself in a position to learn and begin doing what it will take to truly live the life style you want.

First, you will want to read through and complete this Book. At the end of each chapter, I will be giving you action steps that you can use to get you moving towards your goals. These are small steps to get you off your butt, off the couch and help you start getting real estate deals coming in. At the end of this book I will show you where you can get a 30 day action plan that will help to guide you on your path to success. I want you to start using the strategies you have found in this book today.

My Goal is to give you some easy to follow steps that gets you moving in the right direction. This Book should be able to answer most of the questions you have or will point you in the right direction to get your questions answered.

My system is designed for anyone who needs a clear road map on how to start making money in real estate investing.

About the Author

Christopher Seder is a real estate investor located who is based out of small town Montana. He has proven that anyone can become successful in real estate investing no matter where they live.

Christopher received a business degree from Montana State University-Billings. After college, he realized that the job industry sucked, working a job was not for him. Christopher knew if he wanted to live the life of his dreams, he needed to learn how to create financial freedom. And the best way to create financial freedom was to learn from someone who had already done that.

Christopher decided to go into the family business which was real estate investing. His father has been flipping houses and buying rental property for over 30 years and has been involved in over 1200 real estate transactions. Christopher started out helping manage and fix up rental property. Soon after gaining experience and education Christopher and his father started up Big Sky Property Solutions LLC. Big Sky Property Solutions LLC has grown into one of the top real estate investing companies in the Billings Montana area. They wholesale, rehab and buy rental property. Christopher has quickly become a well-known wholesaler and rehabber in his hometown market.

After having success with real estate investing, people started asking Christopher if he could teach them how to get started on doing the same thing. This inspired Christopher to write the book, "Real Estate Flipping Secrets"(now known as NO BS Flipping) which he uses to train new students. He has also created several products such as "Vacant House Riches," "RealEstateVIPCoaching.com," and many more.

Christopher Seder is a Real Estate Investor, Author, Real Estate Coach and Internet Marketer.

Christopher's goal is to provide the best products and services for real estate investors all over the country. You can really tell that Christopher has a passion for real estate investing and loves helping others. Christopher loves helping others capitalize on real estate investment opportunities.

For more info on the author go to **ChristopherSeder.com**

Chapter 1

Getting Started and Finding your Niche

"I can't give you a surefire formula for success, but I can give you a formula for failure: try to please everybody all the time"

-Herbert Bayard Swope

Getting started in real estate investing can be one of the biggest challenges for a new investor. Getting that first deal under your belt is always the hardest. Have you been trying and failed? Don't worry, 99% of people trying to get into real estate investing failed. I am going to address this topic more in a later chapter. The reason most people fail in real estate investing is because they do not realize that it takes time to gain education, experience and confidence. Success does not happen overnight like most people think.

You my friend are different from the 99%, I can tell that you want to succeed and you are going to pay your dues to make it happen.

As you may already know, the real estate market across the nation is in a so called recession. House prices are at an all-time low and investors are buying up property left and right. The best part is that there are enough deals out there for every investor to do hundreds of deals each year.

What is the secret to finding all the deals you can handle? Well, this eBook is going to show you and give you a step by step system for flipping houses in the current economy.

Why do you want to read this Book and learn from me? First off, I have grown up around real estate investors my whole life and my business partner, mentor and my father has been involved in over 1200 transactions and has been in the real estate investing business for over 30 years. In fact, he has given me valuable advice and ideas for this Book. Some of the chapters have been written by him. For years now, he has been collecting rental property and flipping several houses every year.

If you think you can learn something from someone who has been in the business for 30 years then you are right. He is the one that encouraged me to write this after I started having success in real estate. My father is a man that is always looking for different ways to become financially free and real estate has been his ticket. He is also the biggest advocate for education, and has gone with me to many seminars and to learn from best real estate investing coaches in the U.S.

I am not a Guru or an I am not a professional writer. I am an average Joe real estate investor who loves to share what he has learned.

I know the frustration people have with getting started. I have been in your shoes, even with a father who has been doing this for 30 years, getting started is tough. I had to take time to educate myself.

Before graduating from college, I didn't even know what a mortgage was. I know it's sad; I was more focused on golf and having fun with friends growing up. After college, I started to become more interested in real estate investing and creating financial freedom.

How did I go from not knowing what a mortgage was to writing this eBook?

I went to several seminars, read every book I could get my hands on and started working for my dad. I worked as one of his handy men, helping fix up rentals and work on his house flips. I also took a part time job doing foreclosure inspections for a company contracted with various banks. This allowed me to drive around all day long and look for vacant houses.

After I spent 6 months educating myself, my dad and I decided it was time that I started my own real estate investing business with him as a partner.

I have only been in the business for around 4 years now, and I am currently building my rental portfolio 20 ++ and Growing and flipping several houses a month. What I am sharing with you in this Book are concepts and strategies that work in Today's Market. The strategies are working for me, an investor who is learning and growing his real estate business. I want to help you learn and grow too.

Learning the Game

Knowledge is Power. Education is so important in real estate investing. Real estate investors with the most knowledge and then apply their knowledge are the most successful. You need to always be seeking new and improved ways to make your business better and make yourself more profitable. To stay on top in any field, you must be continually looking for new information.

 I am always reading books on real estate investing, motivational books, marketing books and anything that will help me grow as a person and Entrepreneur.

I am here to share with you one of the best and easiest ways to become financially free. They did not teach you this stuff in school, or at least my school never taught it.

What is Real Estate Flipping?

Most people think that flipping houses is simply buying a property, fixing up and then reselling it. But there is so

 much more to Flipping houses than just that. You can flip a house in one hour, 3 months, 5 years or even 20 years. I consider flipping houses finding cheap properties and making a

profit. I am here to tell you that there are several different strategies you can use to make a profit.   You can do this if you have 0 dollars (it might take more work), or you can do this if you have lots of money.

What is the Best Real Estate Investing Strategy to Get Started?

I hear people saying this all the time. Where do I start? I want to get into real estate investing and become financially free but there are so many courses out there all teaching something different so where do I start? Should I do rehabs? Short Sales? Rental Property? Wholesaling? Bird Dogging?

How do you go about determining what niche to go into? Well you do some research. Learn about each niche; buy courses, books, and CD's. Ask other investors in your area what is working for them. Most real estate investing strategies are good and have their own benefits and downsides. If you are just getting started, I recommend finding one of the niches that interests you and start with that, become an expert then add other niches as you gain experience.

You also need to ask yourself why you are getting into real estate investing. Is it to provide your family with a better life? So you can retire young and rich? Help Homeowners with their real estate problems? Make your community better? Create Wealth so you can fund your true passion? Or maybe you want to be filthy stinking rich? Whatever the reason is, you need to determine what it is.

You also need to determine what you need now. Do you need lots of Cash right now? Do you need some kind of residual income/Cash flow every month? Once you determine what you are looking for, then you can really determine what niche you need to be in. Some strategies will give you cash right away, while others will give you little cash up front but lots of cash over time.

I say start with wholesaling or being a property scout. Wholesaling will give you more cash than being a property scout but it is a good option to give yourself some experience, with almost zero risk. Both of these strategies can be done with almost no money, just your time and Marketing efforts.

These two strategies will give you some great experience and help you see if real estate investing is what you really want to be doing.

Next I am going to give you a short description of a few real estate investing strategies. This will give you a good idea of what some strategies are about and can help you pick one that excites you.

Wholesaling

What is wholesaling in a Nut Shell?

- All you have to do is to simply find a motivated seller Who Wants to Sell Fast
- Put that house under contract at 40-60% of its Retail Value/ Market Value.
- Mark it up anywhere from $2,000 to $50,000
- Find an Investor buyer and Assign the Contract to him/her
- Then Collect you Check

Sounds Pretty Simple Doesn't it? It really is and all you really need to know how to do is to find motivated sellers  and how to find buyers which is all covered in this book. When wholesaling, you are just assigning your contract to a buyer who will fix up the property, rent the property or even live in it.

For Example: You find a property for $50,000 that needs $10,000 in repairs. The house is worth $120,000 if it was totally fixed up. So you Get that property under contract, and then find a Buyer who will buy that property for

$60,000. Your seller gets $50,000 you get $10,000 and your buyer gets a property at 50% of its Fixed up Value.

Property Scout

Being a property scout is the simplest of the real estate investing strategies. All have to you do is to find someone looking to sell a property at a discount and then refer that lead to another investor who then gives you a referral fee. Most referral fees are $500 or $1,000 dollars.

You just have to make sure that the investor is actually going to pay you. Get them to sign some sort of contract before you give them the lead.

You do nothing but find leads for other investors. This strategy can be used to learn how to market your business with little risk. The only problem is that you will not make much money.

For more information on being a property scout check out

http://realestateflippingriches.com/help-wanted-now/

Rehabbing aka Fix and Flip

Rehabbing houses is buying houses, fixing them up and re-selling them.  This is what most people consider to be flipping houses. You buy a property at a low price; add value by fixing up the property and the make huge sums of money re-selling it.

Rehabbing is a little riskier than wholesaling but can produce you massive amounts of cash.

On average, our rehab projects make us around $30,000 on average. The Marketing strategies we use to find all of our rehabs, wholesales and 99% of our deals are listed in the marketing section. The rehabbing process is pretty simple; the one thing that most investors get confused or scared about is how do I know what all the repairs cost? In the Evaluating deals section, I will show you how we go about determining repair costs.

We will cover rehabbing houses more in depth in a latter chapter. I am also looking into creating a rehabbing course for my students, that will give you everything you will ever need to know about the process.

Short Sales

A **short sale** is when a lender accepts a discount on a mortgage to avoid a possible foreclosure auction or bankruptcy. Instead of buying from a seller, you are purchasing the property directly from the lender for a discount.

For example: A homeowner, who is facing foreclosure, has an existing first mortgage of $150,000. You write an offer to the lender for $100,000 which is accepted as full payment for the loan. This is a **short sale**.

Why are they willing to take such a discount? Several reasons.
First of all, banks do not like excess inventory and bad loans on their books; therefore, if they see an opportunity where they can sell the property without a huge loss, they will do it.

 Secondly, lenders know they could lose a lot more money if the property goes to foreclosure. There are so many fees involved if the property goes to a foreclosure auction. Banks are better off taking the discount beforehand and be finished with the headache of it all.

Investors today are making a killing helping homeowners in trouble do short sales. A short sale investor wholesales the deal or sells it to someone looking to live in the home. It's a pretty good strategy but can take 3 months, 6 months or longer to complete.

Subject To

When you purchase a property 'Subject To', the existing loan stays in your seller's name. In other words, the seller leaves his current loan on his property in place and makes it available for you and then your buyers' use. You become the owner of the property when the seller signs the Grant Bargain & Sale Deed or other State specific device to transfer property.

What you usually do is to give the buyer a few thousand dollars and they leave. You do subject to deals when the payment on the house is reasonable and they have a good interest rate.

You goal is to then either re-sell the property (if there is any equity) or rent the property out with a lease option. You rent the property out for more than what the payment is and get some nice cash flow every month.

Most subject to deals are put together because there is not a lot of equity in the property.   Investors need to have some sort of equity to buy a property but if a seller has a good interest rate, the property may cash flow.

A lot of our Rehab projects are bought subject too. This way we can get into a property and not have to bring a lot of Cash to the table. Learn everything you can about buying property Subject too.

Lease options

A Lease Option is sort of two separate Agreements. A lease is just a standard agreement to rent a house and an option gives someone the right to purchase the home within a specific period of time for a fixed price.

For example: the option agreement could say that you have the right to purchase the home for $130,000 before March 2014. The person selling the option would charge an option fee (whatever you can get, 5k, 10k 20 k).

The buyer or tenant rents the home until they want to exercise their option. People will do lease options for individuals looking for a house but might not have good enough credit to buy currently. The option period gives them time to get their credit score up and gives them the right to buy the property.

Commercial

Commercial Real Estate refers to retail properties, office buildings, shopping centers, hotels, Sky Scrapers, warehouses, manufacturing facilities, apartment complexes – and  vacant land that have the potential for development for these types of buildings. In short, almost any kind of real estate except single-family homes and single-family lots can be regarded as commercial real estate.

Commercial real estate has made lots of people multi millionaire's and Billionaires. Commercial real estate can make you some of the biggest profits, you can flip them or you can rent them out and receive cash flow every month.

I am currently looking to get into some more commercial real estate ventures.

Buying Notes

A Note is a written document that states a promise to pay, and the terms which include the amount, interest rate and length of time in which to fulfill this promise. When you get a mortgage you sign a promissory note with it. The promissory note ensures that you pay back the amount you borrowed.

As the real estate market continues to slow down, and  with foreclosures on the rise in most of the country, lenders are finding themselves overwhelmed with many sub-performing and non-performing loans.

Some Lenders will consider selling the note to you. Buying the Note Straight from the bank can be a better strategy than doing a short sale. Because once you buy the note, you then become the bank. You can choose to foreclosure on the home owner or work out some sort of deal with them and collect payments on your note. You can also forgo the foreclosure and just have them sign a deed in Lou to you could give the home owners a little bit of cash to vacant.

It's a great investment strategy that is worth looking into.

Mobile Homes

I love Mobile Homes. Most people I know say they despise mobile homes and do not know why anyone would mess with them. Mobile homes do get a bad rap, most think mobile homes are for white trash.   But I will say they are not.

Mobile homes are just cheap houses not on a foundation and you can buy them for dirt cheap. Mobile homes do not take any more work than a regular house. Sometimes you have to move them but that can cost less than $2,000.

You can buy a mobile home for $4,000, put $2,000 in it, so your total investment is $6,000. Then you sell it to a Buyer for $13,000 on a contract with $2,000 down, 10% interest and collect payments every month. In less than a year you have your money back and cash flow every month.

We have a mobile home park where we buy mobiles for less than $10,000 and rent them for $450 - $600. Talk about great cash flow.

Land Lording

Do you want to be king of the slum lords? Good because you do not have to. You can find houses in nice neighborhoods rent them out and make great cash flow every month.

Being a land lord can be a lot of work but well worth it when you have 50 rentals giving you $20,000 +++ in cash flow every month.

I am currently Building my rental portfolio, this is your ticket to financial freedom.

My suggestion for you is to do a Rehab or two and some wholesales then put the money you make into rental property.   Just make sure you have some cash in the bank in case your rental needs repairs or you cannot find a tenant for an extended period of time. With proper planning you should have no problem with rentals.   They will help you retire early and have cash flow to fund your dream life style.

Pros of Real Estate being a Land Lord and Renting Houses:

- Long term wealth creation with the mortgage being paid down
- Appreciation sending the value higher
- Monthly passive cash flow potential
- Huge tax advantages
- Solid property manager can relieve the astute investor from daily management roles

What Strategies do I use?

The Strategies I do are Wholesaling, Buy and Hold (aka Land Lord) and Fix and flip. I also buy Mobile Homes to fix up and Rent out or Re-Sell.

I am only going to cover in a lot of depth the strategies I use. I do not know enough about the other strategies to write a book on. But a lot of my processes for evaluating deals, and marketing can be applied to all the strategies above.

If you are looking for more resources, check out different courses look up RealEstateFlippingRiches.com. Also get on my email list, I am always recommending amazing courses.

Action Steps:

1. List out what your Goals in Real Estate Investing are. What do you want to achieve? Why are you getting in Real Estate investing? How much Money do you want to make in the next year?
2. Pick one of two of the strategies that most interest you? Find out who the top experts in those niches are. Even if wholesaling does not interest you, I suggest that you do some wholesales. This book will show you how get started wholesaling.

Chapter 2

The Most Important Chapter of Your Life

"What we can or cannot do, what we consider possible or impossible, is rarely a function of our true capability. It is more likely a function of our beliefs about who we are."

-Anthony Robbins

Yes this is a Book on Real Estate Investing but before you can become successful at real estate investing, you have to train your mind to be successful.

I hear you whining! Stop whining! This chapter is going to make you rich. I would be doing you an injustice if I did not include a chapter in this book to help you make your life better.

The whole point to real estate investing is to make money, create financial freedom and live the lifestyle you want. You are not going to have success on this earth without first conquering the battle in yourself.

Life is hard. It's so hard that sometimes people get beat up so bad they quit. Life is constantly pulling us down in the dirt. Are you the one who stays down or do you have what it takes to get back up? Listen to what I am saying. You Must Fight For Your LIFE!

You have what it takes to make it, I believe in you. It's not enough to just go through life like a ZOMBIE and allow whatever thoughts that come into your head control you. Do not allow weak feelings to control you or allow the world to have its way with you.

There are millions and millions of those people all over the world. The world seems to love those types of people. You can just point them in a direction and they will follow. Just like ZOMBIES, going through their life lost.

You my friend, are not going to be included in those types of people. Most people do not bother to make themselves better.

They wake up, chug down their coffee, and head off to the job they hate and just go through the motions, come home still in a daze, and watch some depressing TV to escape from their life. It's So Sad.

My Mission and your mission should be to inspire these people. To offer them and show them there is a better way to live life.

Life is too short and we have got lots to accomplish. You are put on this earth for a reason and for a purpose. Only you can discover your purpose and live life to the fullest. You have to Dig deep, look beneath the surface and start asking yourself what is your mission in life.

There is something very important that you need to do and it's your job to figure out what that is. This is what separates average men from Great men. Everyone has the ability to look deep in and find that purpose.

Ok, so this is a book on real estate investing. Why am I saying all of this?

If your head is not screwed on right and if you do not possess a positive attitude and have an optimistic outlook on life, you will not survive and will not thrive at the top level which is where I want you to be.

I also believe that 98% of your success will result from you having a positive attitude. I can tell you almost everything I know about real estate investing and how to make your business successful but if you do not have a positive attitude, we are both wasting our time. I also believe it's more than just a positive attitude. You need to improve in all aspects of your life. I am always trying to make myself better. I know several areas in my life that I need to work hard on. If you improve the aspects of life that I will be talking about later in this chapter, you my friend, will become a money making, successful machine.

To make it in this life you have to be 100% convinced that you can do anything if you really want to.

Do you currently believe that? Every successful person I know has this mindset. As you decide to grow your business you must believe 100% that you are going to succeed. Know that you and your business are the best and going to become the greatest business in your niche.

Life demands a lot from us. It is up to us to train ourselves to become champions. Most professional athletes do not become Super Bowl, World Series or Championship winners without doing things other people are unwilling to do. They train almost all year round, perfecting their bodies and minds to become the best at their sport. We need to train our minds to become great champions in our respected businesses and in life.

How bad do you want financial freedom, have a huge successful business and become the man or woman you have always wanted to be. Take a few moments and really think about what you want in life. Most people skip this small very important step. What do you want?

I have a vision board on my wall that shows everything I want. I have business and personal goals. You should see all the crazy things I currently have on it.

Now we are going to talk about what I believe are the keys to living a fulfilling life. If you learn how to do each of the following, there is no reason you will not live the life you have always dreamed of. Have more success that you have ever imagined and just get the most out of your time here on Earth.

Discover your purpose

I wanted to share with you some things that have changed my life before you even move on any further with your business. I want to share with you the keys that have super charged my life and success. I work on all of these every day.

Your main job should not be your business. Instead it should be growing as a person. How can you get stronger, physically and emotionally? How can you get yourself strong enough so that life does not kill you?

"Don't ask yourself what the world needs. Ask yourself what makes you come alive and then go and do that. Because the world needs people who come alive"

Howard Thurman

What makes you come alive? What's your deepest darkest desire and passion? How bad do you want it? How bad do want it? How bad do you want it?

"Desire is the starting point of all achievement, not a hope, not a wish, but a keen pulsating desire"

Marie Andretti

If you want to become a rock star at anything you chose to do you have to want it bad. So bad that it may drive you crazy at times. The one who wants something most will ultimately get that which he desires.

You will also have to love what you do. A combination of desire and passion is a key to living a full life. If you do not love what you are doing then you will soon give up or just go through the motions. If you love what you are doing then you should have no problem paying your dues and putting in the necessary work it takes to build a multi-million dollar business.

Determination

"Desire is the Key to motivation, but its determination commitment to an unrelenting pursuit of your goal and commitment to excellence that will enable you to have the success you seek"

-Napolean Hill

How determined are you to succeed?

Many people in the real estate investing business fail because they don't keep pushing themselves. They try and try for a few months and don't have any success so they give up. Everyone who is supposed to be successful goes through a testing period where they have to push and push in order to become rewarded with success. Never let one little failure keep you from achieving your ultimate dreams.

You have to put your foot down and say enough is enough. I am going to succeed and do it now.

Self-Discipline

"Disciplining yourself to do what you know is right, important, although difficult, is the high road to price esteem, and personal satisfaction."

Brian Tracy

You have to be disciplined and get yourself in a routine every day that will help you move towards your goals. And by routine I mean pushing yourself to do new things and get out of your comfort zone. We have to do things over and over again. Never do something once and just figure that is good enough. If you want to succeed in life you have to keep doing things over again, things that cause you pain and things that move you towards you goal.

I never feel like doing some of the things that I know are going to bring me to success but guess what, I sacrifice and do it.

When you start something new, you feel some sort of resistance to doing everything that is worth doing. It's the warrior and champions that are willing to give their life for what they want. You feel that resistance to work; the successful feeling and do it anyway. Play it out in your mind what's going to happen if you do not do it. And what's going to happen if you do.

Positive Attitude

I believe that having a positive attitude is key to success. Having a positive attitude rubs off on everyone around you. No one wants to be around someone with a negative attitude.

I also believe that having a positive attitude and believing that you are the greatest is another key becoming successful at whatever you want in life.

Read everything you can get about having a positive attitude.

Motivation

"People often say that motivation does not last. Well neither does bathing, that's why we recommend it Daily"

– Zig Ziglar

Know what motivates you toward success. This is why I recommend everyone write down their goals. Know what you want to achieve and create an action plan of how you are going to achieve them. Be outrageous with your goals and put down your wildest dreams in some of your goals. Update your goals, a year down the road we may not want the same things. I recommend that you don't just shove your goals into your desk. Have them out and posted on your wall where you can see them. Read them every day so that you know why you are working so hard.

The Reason Most people do not have motivation is because they just don't care. Do you care about your future and your goals? Do you care about what you are doing? If you do not then you have no motivation.

Also, fear is a motivator. Fear that you are not going to make it, fear that you are going to lose your business, fear that you're not going to be able to eat. All the successful people have some fear that is driving them.

Hard Effective Work

Success is not handed to anyone. It is given to those who put in the time and energy to get it. You have to push yourself every day and work your ass off. Do what brings in the most money. Do not spend your day working hard doing mundane tasks that never bring you any closer to your goals and dreams.

Some people think that multitasking is a huge skill. I say don't do it. It is best to put all your energy into one thing at a time. This will make you more effective and you will do a better job.

At the end of every work day, you should also prepare a to-do list for the next day. This is important so you can keep on track and move towards your goals. It also makes sure that you have things to do every day to help you stay productive.

You should have a sense of urgency in everything you do. Do not put off your tasks. Most people put off tasks till the last moment or put them off forever. Stop the procrastination and do it right away.

This book that you are reading right now only happened because of this. My friend and I were talking about. I decided to just take action and do it, and the key was just getting it going.

Integrity-don't do business with Liars

You must always keep your words. If you don't keep your word, people won't trust you and will not want to do business with you. Simple enough. Don't do business with people who don't keep their words. Distance yourself from those types of people.

Boldness and Risk taking

The world does not reward someone who is not bold and does not take risks. You have to just ask for what you want and don't take no for an answer. Do not be shy when it comes to what you want.

> "Screw it; Lets do it"
> -Sir Richard Branson

You should also take risks and never be afraid to fail. You have to get out of your comfort zone. You don't grow by doing the same thing, the only way to grow is to try new things and have new experiences.

Energy

> "The key is not to manage time. It's to manage your energy"
> -Tony Schwartz

Everyone should be getting at least 7-8 hours of sleep per night. It has been proven that with less sleep over time you cannot function at 100%. You become less productive and have less motivation.

Exercise is a must for anyone wanting to gain energy. From personal experience I feel energized after every time I work out. I also feel better about myself after every work out. Any when you feel better about yourself, it shows. You have more confidence; you are more enthusiastic and just feel alive.

If you want to start working out I would recommend doing some light work outs for thirty minutes in the morning. Jumping jacks, Lunges, pushups, crunches and a few other simple things to start out, then you can move on to more intense working out. Seek out a personal trainer to help you set up a program specific to your body type and goals.

Action Steps

1. Watch the Secret

2. Buy everything by Anthony Robbins

3. Always be reading some sort of motivational book that makes you feel good.

4. Read or listen to "Secrets of the Millionaire Mind" T-Harv Eker

5. Get rid of negative friends or limit your exposure to them.

6. Be Positive

7. Daily Affirmations – Put a list together of inspiring phrases (example below)

-I am a champion
-I am a world Beater
- I can do anything
-Nothing Can Stop Me
- I am the biggest and best real estate investor around
-I was destined for greatness

8. Start exercising and eating organic

Chapter 3

The Foundation of Your Business:

Marketing for Deals and finding Leads

"Nobody can give you freedom. Nobody can give you equality or justice or anything. If you're a man, you take it"

-Malcolm X

Marketing is the foundation of your business and the most important part of a successful real estate investing business. If you want to be a big time real estate investor, you need to become a big time marketer. The only way to find real estate leads is to market your business.

Leads and deals don't just fall in your lap, some might, it does happen but it will be because people know what you do, which is to buy houses. When you have done a good job marketing yourself and your business, you should have leads coming in like crazy.

The Goal is to let everyone in your community know that you buy houses, close quickly and can pay all cash.

I am a big time student of marketing and believe that we are all one great marketing piece away from getting whatever we want in life.

Study other great marketers and do what they are doing. Study Joe Vitale, Dan Kennedy, and Preston Ely.

All of the marketing strategies listed below are ways to market your business and places you can find real estate leads.

Networking

Get out there and make some friends. To be successful, you have to hand your card out to everyone. Make sure you have cards for your real estate business made up. And not cheap cards get some good cards that stand out and let people know what you do.

Networking and handing out cards can be one of the biggest challenges ever. I don't enjoy meeting new people; I would rather just sit at home. It's a lot easier to just sit at home and watch TV.

I have realized that if I want to become successful, I need to put new habits in place and get out of my comfort zone.

Networking helps you find leads and also grow as a person. Networking really gets you out of your comfort zone. Asking people if they know of a house you can buy is a great way to get over your fear of talking to strangers. I know your mother always said *do not talk to strangers*. She will understand when you show her a $30,000 check.

It's really not as hard as you think. It will take practice and trial and error, to get it down. I ask everyone I meet, even at McDonalds, if they know someone looking to sell their house fast or if they know of anyone who needs to sell. Sounds simple doesn't it?

Make yourself up a few little pitches to say to people and practice them. Practice them in the mirror, on family members and on your dog.

Then go out and do it. You will chicken out a few times; I have chickened out 50 times in a row.   Every person I have given a little pitch too has taken my card. Some give me a weird look at first but everyone has took my card and said they would let me know if they ever heard of anyone who is looking to sell fast.

Here is a Process for Your Networking.

1. Get Business Cards.
2. Get a Google Voice Phone Number (can forward to your phone) this way sellers are calling that number and not your personal phone number.
3. Leave business cards on Boards at Gas stations, restaurants, bars, bathroom stalls, everywhere someone can find one.
4. Hand out cards every time you have the chance to talk to someone.   Ask them if they know of a house you can buy, you are looking to buy a few rentals or fixer uppers and were wondering they knew of anyone looking to sell.
5. Join and attend your Local Real Estate Investors association. This is a group of likeminded real estate investors and gives you a good chance to find deals from them, learn what is working in your market.
6. Find a Master Mind or networking group in your Area. (Business Network International

www.BNI.com) I am a member of a Small Mastermind group that meets twice a month. We discuss problems in our business, our goals, success that we are having, and help each other out.

So who else should you network with?

- Wholesalers (I will address Investor Networking Later on)
- Advanced Investors
- Beginning Investors
- Realtors
- Contractors
- Title Companies
- Mortgage Brokers
- Hard Money Lenders
- Foreclosure Attorneys

All of these people can help you find real estate deals but they are also vital to helping you with other aspects of your business. I have meet lots of these people at my local Chamber event. It's a great place to network with professionals and find Bankers, attorneys and business owners.

If you're going into rehabbing houses, you need to have several good contractors you can call to give you bids and work on your projects.

Finding a Rock Star Realtor

Your Rock Star Realtor Has Arrived!

Every real estate investor needs several amazing realtors to work with. Realtors are consistently getting calls from people looking to sell. Sometimes they come across people who are Super motivated and would be a great candidate for you.

You need to network with tons of Realtors; you need to have a realtor who is sending you lead's all the time. But you also want a realtor who knows what a good deal to you is, this is important.

I have had realtors who would call me about a hot new property that just came on the market, I would get all excited. Then I would find out the sellers are asking $5,000 less than what the property is worth. That's not a deal, why are you bugging me with this. I then have to explain (for the 3rd time), Dude I am an Investor I buy property at 50% of the ARV.

Some realtors will not get it but when you find the realtors who do, you will have lots of success. Always ask your realtor if they have worked with investors in the past and if they are willing to make low offers.

At your first meeting, show your realtor what you are trying to do, paint him or her a picture.

Say you are buying property to fix up and re-sell and looking to make $30,000 or more on each deal.   You can only buy deals that have equity in them.

If you are interested in doing short sales, tell your realtor what type of short sale deals you are looking for.

Bandit Signs

Bandit signs are simply little plastic or cardboard signs that you put up. Just write on the signs "I buy Houses in Ca$h, your phone number and your web site".

I put out bandit signs all over different neighborhoods. Put them up near intersections, near Wal-Mart, Lowes, Home Depot, and anywhere that gets lots of traffic.

Most towns hate bandit signs. I was threatened by the Code Enforcement to stop putting them up or I would be fined so I don't use them as much. If your town is not as strict with them, feel free and put them up.   You can go to www.Banditsigns.com

Flyers

Flyers are one of the cheapest and most effective ways to advertise. The only trouble with flyers is taking the time to put them out. What I do is post flyers all over my downtown area, I post them at bars, restaurants, grocery stores and where ever I can find a bulletin board. You would be surprised at how many places have bulletin boards.

Beat Foreclousre Today!

Free Secrets to Stop Your Foreclosure

End the Stress and Save Your Credit, Free Info at
www.YourWebSite.com

I'll Buy Your House Today!!!!

Transfored? Bad Tenants? Need Fast Cash?
Behind on Payments? House Vacant? Moving?
Making Double Payments? Divorce? Estate Sale?

House Simply Wont Sell?

Here is your Quick and Easy Solutions

-Fast Closing
-Instant Debt Relief
-Cash!!!!

Written offer in 24 hours

Call: (555) 555-5555

www.YourSiteHere.com

Behind on Mortgage Payments?

In Jeopardy of Losing Your House and Hurting Your Credit?

We CAN HELP!
We Buy Houses and Can Close in less than 7 Days

Call the Problem Solvers right now

(555) 555-5555

or Visit

www.YourSiteHere.com

We Buy Houses Cash

Dear Propery Owner,
Do you own an Unwanted propertry and need to Sell Quickly? Does your House need Repairs? Are You Behind On Payments? Facing Foreclosure? Lost your job? Inherited and Unwanted propery?

These Problems Can Happen to Anyone
We Pay Cash for houses and can close quickly

Leave Your Worries Behind! Call today

(555) 555-5555
or Visit

www.yoursitehere.com

We Buy Houses CA$H

Any Area
Any Condition

Quick Closing, Fast Cash

Are You Marking Payments on a House you Can no longer afford?

Beind Transferred?

Making Double Payments?

Facing foreclosure?
Did You Inherit an Unwanted Property?
Getting Divorced?

No Equity? No Problem!
We Can Help!

Call (555) 555-5555 or www.YouSite.com

FREE E-Book Reveals

"How to Sell Your House in 10-30 Days.... Even if your House has been on the Market for Months"

Learn the secrets realtors do not want you to know about home selling.

www.YourSiteHere.com

Vehicle Signs

Have you ever seen a car driving down the street with a Big "WE BUY HOUSES CASH" sign on it? You can get nice car signs from VistaPrint.com or other sign makers. Search for Door Magnets or Car door signs on Google.

My signs are magnetic so I can easily take them off whenever I want. I get leads all the time from someone saying they saw my car sign at Wal-Mart or driving around town.

Or you could go with a Van like the one below. Park that in front of a house you are remodeling or park it at Lowes when you are picking up supplies. Leads will come in like crazy.

Banners and Billboards

Banners and Billboards have been around for what seems like ever. If you have the $500 - $1000 per month to use Billboards use them. They are great ways to brand your business and get the word out. I do not use them because I like to keep my marketing expenses down.

Banners are another way to get the word out. Above is an example of a banner ad that you could use. Hire some out of work protesters to hold up your signs. They will get attention and some calls or web site hits.

The Number 1 Way we Market our Business!

Direct Mail

Direct Mail is one of my favorite ways to market and one of my most effective strategies. If you want to be successful as a real estate investor, you need to be doing some kind of direct mail campaign.

Direct mail campaigns can cost very little and the best part you can see how effective your letter is would be on the amount of responses you get back. Its very important to always track your direct mail responses to make sure your letter is being effective.

Direct mail campaigns should be the corner stone of your marketing efforts. It does take work to get the letters out every week but there are ways to outsource your labor and automate the process.

Here is a list of Mailers I send out.

- **Pre-Foreclosure**- Get the list from Title Companies or Clerk and Recorders office
- **Probate**- Court House (probate profits course)
- **Evictions**- Court house

- **Divorce-** I compile my list from the Legal Paper here. I then look up if they own any type of property on the county assessors web page.
- **Tax Lien Lists- Court house**
- **Bankruptcy Attorneys-** Google
- **Probate Attorneys** - Probate cases (refer to my Probate profits eBook)
- **Code Violations** - Your County or City Code enforcement
- **Realtors-** Look at the MLS to see who is Selling the Most
- **Out of State Owners-** Buy the List
- **Investor lists-** MLS look up people who have closed on more than one property the past year and people who have paid cash for real estate.

You need to educate yourself on where you get the lists in your area. Most of my lists come from the county court house, some places you can get access to court house records online. I can compile a few of the lists I need straight off the counties web site but for evictions and probate, I will have to go to the court house. You can also get just about any list you need on listsource.com.

I recommend that you do the mailers yourself first and document everything you do. Then later on, hire someone for $9 an hour to do the work for you. Just always make sure you have detailed instructions that a 3 year old could understand. I currently have a lady and her husband who hand address, stamp and stuff all of my mailers for $10 per 50 envelopes. I highly recommend you find someone who can do this for you when you can afford it.

You will also want to learn to create a great letter to send out. Having a letter that gets people to call is important. It's pointless to send out a letter that gets no responses. I have included one of my letters, use it or change it. I am always tweaking my letters and still trying to find the best letter possible.

Steps

1. Create Your Killer Letter
2. Compile Your Lists
3. Print off Your Mail Pieces.
4. Mail Your Letter or Post Card
5. Answer Your Phone

My Super-Secret Weapon

The yellow letter has become the super-secret weapon a lot of real estate investors are using to get a higher than average response rate on their direct mail campaigns.

So what is the yellow letter? It is hand wrote on yellow notebook paper.

Here is an example.

Dear Home owner,

Hi My Name is Christopher Seder and I would like to $ BUY$ Your property Located at 1234 Seller Lane please Call

(406) 555-5555
Thanks

Christopher

This letter makes it seem like you are just a regular JOE who is curious about purchasing a property.   Use this letter I guarantee it will work better than any professional looking letter.

MLS Listings (Multiple Listing Service)

The MLS is one of the things real estate agents use to advertise their property. Most of the properties listed on the MLS are retail properties but you will find great deals on REO's on the MLS and there are motivated sellers on the MLS.

One trick I do is to print out all the listings that have been on the MLS for 6 months or longer. I check for price drops and if a property has dropped a lot over the past few months, then I know the seller has some motivation. I will then send the real estate agent involved an offer on the property.

Most of the properties that are listed on the MLS are on http://Realtor.com. I would check there first and you would also want to have the realtor you work with look up property for you on the MLS.

Look for houses on these sites that may need work and also look for houses that have been listed for over 6 months. When houses are listed for over 6 months, sellers tend to become extremely motivated.

On the MLS I also look for expired listings. These are listing that had been on the market for a long time and never sold. When this happens, the sellers may still want to sell and are frustrated because their realtor could not get their house sold.

Have your realtor do a search for all expired listings in the past 3 months, 6 months or however long you want to go back.

HUD **and Foreclosure Sites**

There are several sites that list REO's (bank owned property).   You can find some of the best deals on houses from Banks.

Finding bank owned property is becoming easier and easier.   You will be provided with several web sites below that list Bank Owned Property.

www.HUDHomeStore.com

What is a HUD Home?
A HUD home is a 1-to-4 unit residential property acquired by HUD as a result of a foreclosure action on an FHA-insured mortgage. HUD becomes the property owner and offers it for sale to recover the loss on the foreclosure claim

https://va.equator.com/

This is the Site to find VA foreclosed home. VA is the Veterans Affairs. This is the site to find houses that had VA loans and have fallen into foreclosure.

Foreclosure.Com

Foreclosure.com is a site that has all of the foreclosures listed. The site is a paying site, but if you are serious about finding foreclosures, I would check it out and try out their FREE trial to see if the site is for you.

RealtyTrac.com

The company's mission is to make it easier for consumers, investors and real estate professionals to locate, evaluate, buy and sell properties. RealtyTrac is the only major real estate website to feature foreclosure, auction, bank-owned, for-sale-by-owner, and resale properties.

Other places to check are bank web sites. Most Banks list some of their REO's on their own web site. You can check Bank of America, Chase, Wells Fargo and all the banks that you can think of.

Bank of America

http://realestatecenter.bankofamerica.com/

Property Management Companies

Property Management companies are great places to find leads. Property management companies manage rentals for land lords. These companies could have 10, 100, or 1000 land lords they manage property for.

Sometimes land lords get fed up with dealing with tenants and want to liquidate their property. They will usually notify their property management company, that they are selling their property and will no longer need their services.

Get in good with owners or the secretaries of these companies.   See if you can get a list of land lords from them or if they will notify you when a property owner is thinking about selling.

I always let them know that if I buy a rental from a lead they gave me, I will let them manage the rental for me. Even if I am not going to, I want them to feel like they will get my business.

To get a list of property management companies in your area, simply Google "Your Area Property Management", look at the Google Places listing for all the companies.

Foreclosure and pre-foreclosure Inspectors

Did you know that there are companies out there contracted with Various Banks to do foreclosure inspections for them? These inspectors drive around all day and take pictures of houses where the home owners are 30, 60, and 90 days late or more on their mortgage payment.

I know this because I got a job from a company doing these inspections in my area. I was doing 300-400 inspections a month. Isn't that a list that you would love to have?

What you could do is try to find property inspectors in your area and ask if you can buy their list from them.

While I did the inspection, I didn't really get into trying to help a lot of these people because of it conflicting with my job but I did send mailers to some of them. I also helped some get loan modifications and save their houses.

With this list, you can really get a jump on your competition.

Land Lords Running Classified Ads

I have found a couple of deals by sending mailers to or responding to Land lords running classified ads on craigslist and in the paper. I have also added several names to my buyers list by doing this. If they say "no I am not looking to sell", I switch up the conversation and ask if they are looking for more rental property.

A lot of times, these land lords are frustrated with bad tenants and would much rather sell their property.

Driving for Dollars

I have found some of my very best deals while driving for dollars. You need to be on the lookout for vacant houses and fixer uppers every time you leave your house.

When driving around looking at houses, you are looking for signs that a property is vacant or in distress. These signs include over grown grass, weeds, boarded windows, newspaper on the door step, Notice of trustee on the door (just a white piece of paper on the door), a house that looks trashy, and needs work.   The best way to determine if a house is vacant is by looking into the window. If there is nothing inside, I would say the house is vacant.

After you have located a vacant property, go to the counties tax assessors' web site or office and look up the property address. There, you can find out who owns the property and sometimes it will give you a current address. Then, simply send them a letter (my super-secret yellow letter).   For more information and a full course on driving for dollars go to **VacantHouseRiches.Net**

Calling For Sale by Owners

I am always looking for FSBO signs in yards. The best deals I have found have been from people trying to sell their home on their own. You can also look in your local paper for ads or go online. Simply type in FSBO and your area in Google and Hundreds of sites will come up.

Some popular Sites

- www.FSBO.com
- www.Forsalebyowner.com
- www.craigslist.com

Classified Ads

One of my Favorite ways to Market is Classified Ads. I have a classified ad running in a local newspaper that cost me $100 a month and I get 10 or more calls a week from it. A deal that I just closed in around Christmas came from guying calling me from my Classified ad in the paper.

All I simply have is *"Cash Offer for Your House in 7 minutes, my Phone Number and Web Site"*.

You can also have *I Buy Houses*; *Cash for your house*, *I'll Buy your House Today* or Something Along those lines.

The good thing about Classified ads is that you do not really have to do anything. Just post your ad, sit back and let your phone ring.

Online Classified Ads

Another Great Place is to put ads on all the Free Online Classified sites like Craigslist.org, backpage.com and Kijijji (eBay's free Classifieds).

Everyone these days post their property on Craigslist.org. As for me, I post all of my rentals and property I have for sale on Craigslist.org. Whenever I post an ad for my house, I get hundreds of calls.

I also try to post an ad on Craigslist looking for motivated sellers every day or so.   Refer to the Classified ad Riches course to get tons of great information on classified ad marketing.   Go to ChristopherSeder.com for more info.

Action Steps:

- Contact a Local Realtor about Getting MLS Access or Helping You Run Comps
- Browse Your Areas HUD Listing
- Contact 3 FSBO on Craigslist.org
- Start Compiling Probate, Foreclosure and Divorce Mailer Lists
- Sent out 10 yellow letters this week
- Find out when the next REIA meeting is in Your Area.

How to become a Ninja Marketer

"Two roads diverged in the wood, and I took the one less traveled by, and that has made all the difference"

-Robert Frost

Marketing is the most important part of your real estate investing business. I would do you an injustice if I did not tell you a little bit about marketing and show you how to become a Ninja Marketer. Anyone can put an ad up and get some responses but the great marketer can get anyone to take action.

Step 1: You need to realize that you are a direct marketer.

Direct marketing is a form of advertising that reaches its audience without using traditional formal channels of advertising, such as TV, newspapers or radio. Businesses communicate straight to the consumer with advertising techniques such as fliers, catalogue distribution, promotional letters, and street advertising.

Direct Advertising is a sub-discipline and type of marketing. There are two main definitional characteristics which distinguish it from other types of marketing. The first is that it sends its message directly to consumers, without the use of intervening commercial communication media. The second characteristic is the core principle of successful Advertising driving a specific "call-to-action." This aspect of direct marketing involves an emphasis on track able, measurable, positive responses from consumers (known simply as "response" in the industry) regardless of medium.

If the advertisement asks the prospect to take a specific action, for instance, click here for a free e-book or visit a website, then the effort is considered to be direct response advertising.

The Goal in your marketing efforts is to get your prospect to act now as you will only have three seconds to capture their attention.

Step 2: You have to study direct marketing and persuasion

- Frank Kern
- John Carlton
- Dan Kennedy
- Robert Craldini
- Preston Ely
- Joe Vitale

These are all great authors to read about and study. I study all of their work, their sales letters and emails. Study the successful marketers and someday, it will just click and you will get it.

One key to marketing is to take what someone else has already done and copy it. Study what these great marketers are doing, look at their ads, subscribe to their newsletters and try to figure out why their marketing efforts work so well. Use the basic outline for what they are doing in their newsletters, articles and marketing pieces.

I like to save marketing pieces and sales letters that have made me want to buy. I then dissect the sales pieces and try to figure out why they worked on me.

If you want to be the best, you have to learn and copy the best. Copying what other successful people are doing is the key to my success. Preston Ely who is one of the best real estate marketers out there, said that copying others was what made him a great marketer. Do not directly copy them word for word, that is illegal. When I say copy I mean copy their style and the type of marketing they are doing. Do you get what I am saying? I hope so.

Step 3: Practice

Practice makes perfect or something along those lines. The only way to get good at marketing is to get out and practice. Do some experiments and find out what works and what does not. It took me months to find an ad to put on online classified sites that finally worked. I was trying tons of different ads and none of them were getting any response until it just hit me that I was not doing some key marketing principals to get buyers to act now. Want to learn how to get buyers to act now? I will be getting to that in a minute.

Ninja Marketing Tips and Tricks

Rule # 1 in marketing is **DON'T BE BORING.**

You need to be funny, personal and a little outrageous. For some odd reasons, people find outrageous people exciting and are more drawn to them but make sure to be yourself. If you are not an outrageous person, then do not act like one. People can sense when someone is not being truthful and that turns them off even more.

So how do you become funny? Some people are naturally funny. Me I am not naturally funny but I work on it and try to learn how I can become a funnier writer and person. The key to being funny in your writing is, having a surprise or twist. You think the ad is going to go one way but takes a complete 360 degree turn.

Here is an example of a add for a house

"Do not buy this House! I am warning you, if you buy this house you will make tons of money and you will quit your job tomorrow "

Now anyone that reads that ad is going to laugh a little and think it was funny. There is a book called comedy writing secrets. It is going to open your eyes on being funny. It's a pretty good book and if you are really serious, I recommend you read it. It's not the easiest read ever but has useful information in it. It will change your views on comedy and make you a funnier writer.

How to be Outrageous

You have to be boarder line scandalous. Not sleazy or anything but just a personality. Sex sells, there has been research done that a web page with a pretty girl on it gets better results and more leads then one with a random guy on it. What is the lesson there? Get a female on your web page and in your advertising.

You would want to also use emotionally charged words. Words like sex, die, death, words that give people some

 kind of emotional response. Write sentences that when someone reads it they say "I cannot believe he said that".

Kenny Rushing is another good example of this. He is another great real estate investing marketer. I would Google him and watch some of his YouTube videos.

Look at the celebrities that are the most popular. A lot of them are a little crazy. Lady Gaga is huge right now and she dresses outrageously. People like that.

Be Different

Step 1: Take note of what others in your area are doing

Step 2: Do the exact opposite.

If they have fancy web pages, make ugly ones. If they are sending out long emails, send out short ones. If they are sending out letters, send out post cards.

The point in being different is to set yourself apart from your competition. This way people know who you are.

Be Personal

In every letter, or email you send, you need to make the letter seem like you are writing specifically to your customers. You're asking yourself how the heck I do that. Well, act like you are writing a letter to a friend or family member.

Do not use big words that no one understands in your writing and marketing. You want to write so a child could understand what you are saying. I know big words and technical terms look great but if your potential clients have no idea what they mean, they will skip over them or get bored with it and move on.

One thing to do is to always use first names in your marketing. I know you cannot do this with all marketing but if you are doing an email campaign, make sure you have a program that puts their first name in. People love to see and read their name.

Psychological Triggers

These are triggers that get people to act now and want to buy what you are selling. There probably are more of them but these are what I have learned to use in my marketing.

- Reciprocation
  - This is pretty much when we receive a gift from someone, we feel like we need to give them something in return or make it up to them.
- Know/Like/Trust
  - I read somewhere that with everything being fair a person will buy from his friend and with all things being not so fair a person will still buy from their friends.
  - This just means that people would rather do business with their friends, so become friends with your clients and prospects.
- Authority/ Experts
  - People listen to authority figures. You want to become the leading authority or expert in your area in whatever business you are in. How do you do this? Write tons of articles, videos, speak at clubs and soon you will become the expert go to person.
- Scarcity/Urgency
  - This is my favorite and the one I use the most. If you have something that is rare, people would want that more. I always add in all my marketing something that says this offer will not last forever or I am only buying one house. If someone sees that this deal is going to go away soon, they will want to act now; otherwise they may lose out on an amazing opportunity.

- Social Proof
    - You need to have testimonials in your marketing or on your web site. When people see that you have solved a problem for real people, they will be more likely to buy. One testimonial is worth 100 sales pitches. People like to buy because others have bought. Everyone is looking for approval from others.

Newsletter Marketing

A newsletter may seem like something your business may not need but every business could make more money using them. Why would a newsletter help make you more money? It's simple. A newsletter is a way to stay in front of your clients.   Clients sometimes have a short memory and if you can keep in front of them once a month, it will remind them of what you have to offer. Newsletter gives you a chance to show customers new things you are working on or have to offer them.

Always give before you take. It is important to give first before you ask them to do something for you.

So here is my simple format I use when writing a newsletter.

1. Start with a great opening paragraph
2. Talk about something funny that is going on in your life
3. You could also add a joke, or something funny
4. Give them an inspirational quote

5. Picture of the week
6. Whatever you are pitching/your product/wholesale deal
7. Testimonial

8. Tip of the Week

I also like to add in what I am working on and try to be as personal as possible. Above is just an example of how I try to structure my newsletter. Use it if you would like or make your own.

Closing thoughts on marketing

These are just a few of my tips and tricks for you to make your marketing better. I recommend that you study marketing and psychology. A great book for marketing I highly recommend everyone to read is **Hypnotic Writing by Joe Vitale**. It teaches you on how to persuade customers with only your words.

Also get a Book Called *"Influence the Psychology of Persuasion"* is a must read. Influence is a psychology book, I will warn you it is pretty boring but does open your eyes to why your customers will act in a certain way. After you read this book, your eyes and views will be opened. Every time you hear a sales pitch, you will know what they are trying to get you to do.

There are hundreds of other must reads, do some research and find what they are. Use the authors I gave to you earlier.

Always remember to be yourself and have fun with your marketing. Now buckle up, you're in for an exciting ride, next up would be Internet Marketing and how you can get ranked in the search engines.

Action Steps:

- Start Learning about Direct Marketing
    - Get Joe Vitale's Hypnotic Writing Book
    - Get all of Dan Kennedy's Books
- Create a Newsletter template and write your first newsletter. Start writing them monthly or weekly.
-

Chapter 4

Warp Speed
Evaluating Secrets
worth Killing For

"It's far better to buy a wonderful company at a fair price than a fair company at a wonderful price"
-Warren Buffett

Now you have implemented your marketing and your phone is ringing like crazy. People are calling in saying "Hey, I saw that you buy houses? I have a house for sale.

You say great! I just have few questions, and then you go through the lead sheet with him or her.

Being able to quickly and accurately evaluate a deal is one of the most important skills a person can acquire as a real estate flipper. If you are getting hundreds of leads in a month but have no idea how to spot a good deal, then you will not be successful.

It's important to be able to spot a deal from a dud (time waster). I know that when I first started, I spent way too much time talking with sellers who wanted $100,000 more than I could even consider paying for the house.

So Let's Start From the Beginning. You have taken a Call from a Lead. Provided Below is a Lead Sheet. Go through and ask them all the Questions Provided. I have given you sample questions to ask for each.

Sellers will most likely call you and say something like "Hey, I saw your ad saying you buy houses? What's the process? Or how does this work?" I tell them I buy a few houses every month for rentals and also buy a few to fix up and re-sell. The process is simple, I will ask you a few questions about the property, and then determine what I could pay for the property and let you know.

I then go over the lead sheet with them.

Lead Sheet

Contact Information:

(What's the name of the owner on title?, is there more than one person on title?)

Phone Number: Is the Phone number you called with the Best way to reach you?

Email: Do you have an email where I could send you a contract?

Address: What's the Address? City? Zip?

Bed and Bath: How many bed rooms and Bath rooms does the house have? **Square footage:** How big is the house? Square feet? **Year Built**: What year was the house built in?

Construction type: Is the house a Block or Frame house?

Property type: Single Family? Condo, Mobile, Duplex, commercial, Etc

Garage: Is there a Garage?
 Any Special Features? Pool, Hot Tub, Etc?

Is there a Particular reason you are looking to sell?

(I will explain the importance of this below this lead sheet, this is the most important question)

Repairs Needed?

What are all the repairs needed?   (Most sellers will not tell you really what needs to be done)   **I will usually estimate $15,000, until I do a full scope of work.**

Occupancy?

Is the house currently occupied? Who? **If tenant**: What is the Rent and when does the lease expire?

How quickly do you need to sell?

What do you Currently Owe on the Property?

(If the Seller refuses, stop and "Say Mam or Sir, I cannot make you an offer on your property unless I know this, for me to properly evaluate everything, I need to know otherwise I cannot help you)

Are your Payments Current?   If not: How Far behind are you? Who is the Loan with?

Has a foreclosure been filed?

(Only ask if they are late on payments)

What are you looking to get for the property?

(If the sellers will not give you a price, simply say "Ok no problem, could you at least give me a general range of where I need to be so that I do not insult you with")

***If I can offer you cash and pay all your closing cost, what is the least you will accept?

(This is the money statement, always use this)

Once you are done asking them all these questions, simply say "Thank you, I will check this out right away, run some comps and get back to you as soon as possible with my offer.

How easy is that?   Now we can get into looking dissecting the deal and determining if it's a good one.   But let's talk a little about the Sellers Motivation first and why it's the most important thing.

I always ask sellers "Is there a particular reason you are looking to sell"? You really need to find what the seller's motivation is. If the reason for selling is not a very motivated reason, then the deal is usually not going to be a good one.

For Example, *"We are just looking to upgrade our house"* *is not a motivated reason*

A Motivated Reason: *"We are going to Lose our house to foreclosure in a month if we do not get it sold" is a motivated reason*

Another Motivated Season: *"Property needs lots of work and I do not have the money to fix it up"*

We Need to Get the Sellers Motivation because if a seller is really motivated then you know you can deal with them and possibly get the property at a discount. As you may or may not have figured out, we as investors do not pay retail price for a property, we buy houses at a 50% discount or more.

When a Seller is not motivated to sell his property, he or she is less likely to offer discounts as there is no pressure on them to get the house sold.

Looking up Property on the County Tax assessor's web Site

After I have gone over the lead sheet, I like to look at the tax assessors records. This is good for a few reasons.

- I can see who is the owner on title
- See a little description about the property (beds, baths, sq ft)
- I can see how much the taxes are each year

Step 1: Locate your Counties Tax Assessors Web Site.

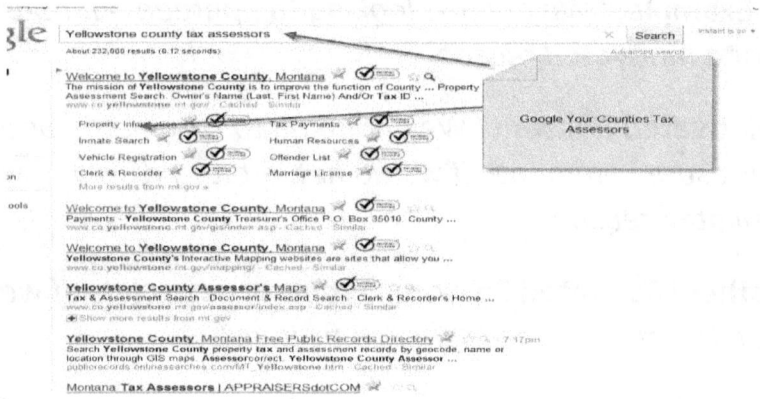

Step 2: Search Your property

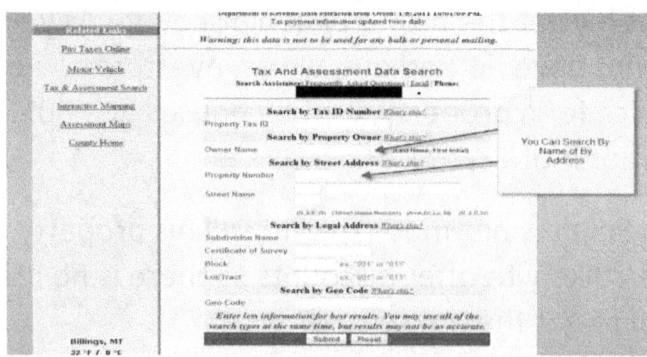

Step 3: Find your property

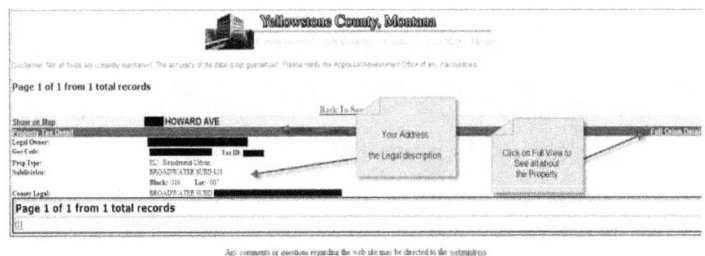

Step 4: Browse the Property Listing

Searching the Tax Assessors is pretty simple. It might take you a little bit to get the hang of it.

Just look for Assessors Value, Beds Baths, Who's on title, year built and whatever you need. You will also need the legal description when filling out a contract.

What is a Good Deal?

Now that we have the lead sheet filled out and determined the seller's motivation, what they are looking to get for the property, and what the least they will take. It's time to see if we have a good deal.

First we have to determine what type of real estate deal we have or what we think is the best way to make money with the deal.

There are several different types of deals out there and several different things you can do with each type.

- Wholesale Deals - Do I want to wholesale this Property? Do I know any rehabbers or land lords who would want this property?
  Do I need Cash Now?
- Fix and Flips – Should I fix this Property Up and Re-sell it? Do I have the Cash to Buy the Property? Could I Get a Loan?
- Rentals- Would this be a good renal for me? Does the Property Cash Flow?
- Retail – Would this house make a Good First time Home buyer house? Is there no work to be done?
- Lease Option – Is there a Market for people to Buy and Rent this Property? Is the seller willing to rent this property for a while?
- Foreclosure/Short Sale – Is there no equity in the Property?

- <u>Commercial</u> – Is this a commercial Property? Could I wholesale to a Commercial Buyer? Could I get a Loan?
- <u>New Construction</u>
- <u>Discounted Notes</u> – Could I Buy the Note?
- <u>Mobile Homes</u> – Rent? Flip?
- <u>Realtor Referral</u> – Does the Home owners want more than I can pay for this? Would they be better going off with a Realtor?

That is a list of a few different types of deals you could come across. You should have some sort of an idea of what these strategies are from chapter 1. Ask yourself the questions above or questions of your own. Ask and you shall come up with your answer. I also ask myself what kind of deal is this? What would be the best way to make money with this deal? You should have an idea of what you are going to do with the deal before you ever close or meet with the seller.

The Only Deals I usually Deal with is Wholesale Deals, Rehabs, Rentals, and Mobile Homes. I am always looking to make a buck so I also refer other leads to other investors and realtors. The reason I refer my deals to other investors is because if they buy that property, they will pay me a referral fee.

The others are good options but I do not feel comfortable doing some. I have not studied them or done a lot of the strategies to become proficient. Maybe one day I will. . Learn about all of the strategies and pick the strategies you like best.

If I come across a deal that I do not want, I usually know what type of deal I have before I get off the phone with the seller. I will say to them *"Thanks, I will evaluate this information and my partner or I will contact you soon"*

The reason I say my Partner is because if I am going to refer the deal out to another investor I do not want the seller to know. I will tell the other investor to come across as a partner of mine or a business associate.

It will take practice to be able to determine if you have a good deal or not while on the phone with the seller.

The Graphic Below gives you a look at all the strategies. They all funnel into your data base where you determine how to make money with your lead.

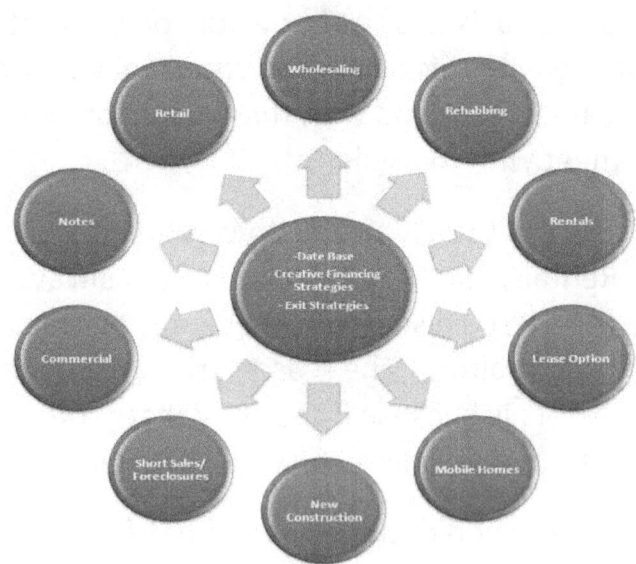

Note: *You should always have your exit strategy figured out before you close on your property or even before you ever meet with a seller. Knowing what type of deal you*

have is a good way to determine exit strategy. Your Exit strategy is just what you are going to do with the property or how you are going to make a buck.

Let's talk about what a good deal is? What do you think a good deal is?

I know a lot of investors fear determining what a property is worth. You say to yourself what if I over pay and get a dud and lose all my money? Then what? Well I am here to tell you that with a simple little process, you will not over pay.

A good deal in every area is really different and all investors look for something different. When buying a property, I like to be around 50% of the Retail Value (value other homes are selling for, to first time home buyers) or After Repair Value (value of house is 100% good condition).

 In rental property, I like to buy houses that will cash in $300 or more a month. That's just me. Some investors will pay more for a property and some will pay less, as long as there is money to be made.

You want to know what the market is doing. In a hot market, you can pay a little more. In a down market, you would want to pay as little as possible.

You also need to look at the neighborhood. We want to buy property in decent neighbors, and not in the worst neighborhood in the town. A Great deal in a bad neighborhood can be a headache. A fair deal in a great neighborhood can make you lots of money.

But here is a simple formula that a lot of investors use and a lot of investor coaches teach their students.

ARV x 70%

Minus Repairs

Minus Closing Cost:

Minus Holding Cost:

Minus Selling Cost:

= Your Purchase Price

That should give you a good estimate of what you will want to pay. Just insert your numbers in and come up with your purchase price or offer. This is for rehab projects.

What are Rehabbers looking for?

Ask other investors what they are willing to pay for certain types of houses. Ask a Rehabber what type of house he is buying and at what price. The best way to really find out if you have a good deal is to ask people who are buying houses right now.

Rehabbers are looking for equity in deals. They are looking to buy a property fix it the property and make $20,000 or more. I know because I do rehabs. It's all about equity in a deal.   You need to have enough wiggle room in a deal for their repair costs, holding cost, loan costs (if they are getting a loan), closing cost and their profit.

Rehabbers want houses that have a sturdy foundation, where they can just go in and not have to do lots of structural work.   Or at least that's what I like. I am sure there are investors who would look at anything. I like a nice house where I can go in and paint, carpet, remodel the kitchen and bathroom and maybe paint or side the outside.

The Left House is NOT what you are looking for; the house on the right is exactly what you are looking for.

What are land lords looking for?

Most land lords, unless they are crazy, are looking for cash inflow and return on their investment.

Land Lords are looking for property that will give them monthly positive income and cash on cash return.   The return on the example below is huge and you may not get that kind of return with most single family homes.

But this example should give you a good idea of how to come up with cash flow and cash on cash return.

In the next section, I will talk about the income Approach to determining a property's value.

Purchased a 14x 70 2 Bed 1 Bath Mobile

Purchased price of $4,000

Repairs of $500

Total Investment $4,500

Rented to a Section 8 tenant (government pays their rent every month, guaranteed rent)

Rented for $500 a month, Lot rent is $140/per month, Taxes and Insurance $25/month

$500 - $140 - $25 = **$335/ month cash flow**

$335 x 12 = $4020/year $4020/ $4500 = **89% return on your Money.**

Methods for Determining Value

The single most important factor in estimating value is Location. Bad locations will never increase much in value over the long term. A good location will always attract new buyers.

Four Characteristics of Value

1. Demand – How many buyers and sellers are in the market
2. Utility- Ability of the property to meet desires
3. Scarcity
4. Transferability- Can a property be sold easily? Will title transfer?

I am going to touch on two approaches to find the value of a property.

1. Direct Sales Comparison Method (Running Comps)
2. Income Approach

The Direct Sales Comparison Method is based on the principle of substitution, which states that the value of a property is based on the cost of purchasing a property of equal desirability and utility.

This method is saying that someone would not pay any more for a house than what it would cost them to buy a similar house.

This approach uses recent nearby, similar home sales to determine what a property is worth.

- Used for residential homes
- Used by realtors
- Comparable sales should be current sales, within 3 months
- Sales most similar to the Subject Property

We are looking to find the fair market value, which is defined as a willing and knowledgeable buyer, in no hurry to buy, buys a property from a knowledgeable seller with now pressure to sell.   Remember, as an investor, we do not pay fair market; we buy houses at a discount but we need to know this as a starting point.

Remember to always compare similar to similar. When comparing houses, you want to look mostly at houses with similar beds and bath rooms.   Compare 3 bed room 2 bath houses to other 3 bed room 2 bath houses. It's a huge jump in price from a 2 bed to a 3 bed but it's not that big of a jump from a 3 bed to a 4 bed.

Here is another good tip. This will help you to determine what houses are worth quickly.

What I like to do is to research specific neighborhoods and find out what an average house in that area is selling for. Once I find what the most common house type is and what the price is, it will make my comp running easier. I still run a full analysis on houses I go and look at but it helps for me to make offers over the phone.

For Example: Let's say a 3 bed room 2 bath on the west end of my town averages $180,000. Then if I get a lead in from a guy who says, "Hey, I have a 3 bed 2 bath on the west end for sale". I can easily know that most 3 bed 2 bath houses in that area are selling for $180,000.

Do you get what I am saying? That's just a quick way to estimate Values. Do this for all the area's that you plan on investing in.

Income Approach

The income approach recognizes that the value of a property is related to the amount of net income the property can produce.   This approach estimates a property's value by calculating the present value of the net

Gross Scheduled Income
-Operating Expenses
= Net Operating Income

Operating Expenses

- Real Estate Taxes
- Utilities
- Insurance
- Property Managers Fee
- Repairs
- Advertising

Capital Improvements, replacement costs, depreciation and interest are not operating expenses.

To determine the value of the property using the income approach, you would want to take the Capitalization Rate for your community divided by the Net operating Income. You can get the Capitalization Rate for your area by calling any local Appraiser.

We only use this method for multi-unit rentals but could be useful for any rental that you want.

When buying a rental, just make sure that if you do buy the property, after all your expensed you will still have some cash inflow every month.

Running Comps

Comps are Comparable Property. These are houses that are similar to the houses you are evaluating in size and style.

To get the most accurate comps, you would want to use the MLS. I like to use houses that have been sold within the past 90 days but sometimes you might have to go a little further back. If you are not a licensed realtor and do not have MLS access, there are other ways to get comps.

Sites that Provide free Sold Comps

- http://www.cyberhomes.com
- http://www.eppraisal.com
- http://www.zillow.com
- http://www.realestate.yahoo.com/re/homevalues/
- http://www.realquest.com
- **http://Freedomsoft-4.com** ← Get it NOW!

These Sites are not the final determinate of as-is or ARV but only for quick reference purposes and to give a general indication and insight. The MLS is the best and most accurate way to go. Get a local realtor to run some comps for you or figure out a way to get access. I recommend that you try and get access yourself because every once in a while, you will need to get your comps right away and a realtor could take a day or more. Good deals and motivated sellers do not always wait around.

When pulling comps, I will usually try to go with the lowest comps that are comparable to my property.   This way, I can protect myself a little and not think my property is worth more than it actually is.

Here is one of the Software tools I use to run quick comps. The Software is called FreedomSoft. It's a data base where you can run comps. It's only available a few times a year for a limited time. If you have a chance, buy it.

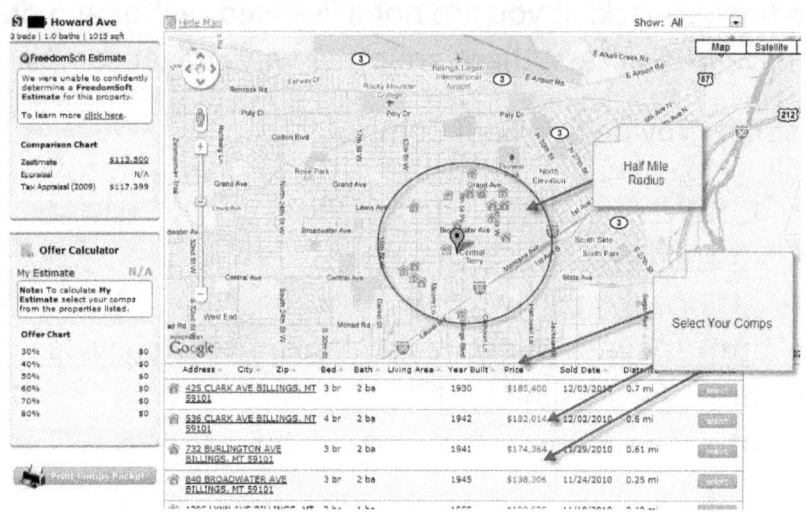

I am a realtor so I have access to the MLS in my area.

Here is how I Run Comps.

1. Do a Quick Search in the MLS data Base
2. In the map area I draw a Circle ½ mile around the Subject house
3. I then enter in my search criteria. (ie, 3 bed, 2 bath, 1800 sq ft)

4. I then do a search for sold houses within the past 90 days.
5. Then I pick out 3 to 5 comps that I feel are the best fit
6. Print them out.

After I have my comps printed out, I usually do a Google Map search of my Subject property to see if I can get a street view of the property. That way I can get a picture of what the house looks like and a view of the neighborhood.

Now you should have a good idea of what your property is worth in 100% great condition.

Note: *What your House is worth is what people are paying for it. Not what's listed. Always go off of sold comps. Current listing only show what other people are trying to sell their houses for or what a realtor thinks a house is worth.*

Estimating Repairs

Because we usually make all of our initial offers over the phone, we never really know exactly how much work the property will actually need.

Here is what I usually estimate

Seller Says No work = around $5,000

Seller Says minor paint and carpet = $10,000

Seller Says Needs work = $15,000

Seller Says Needs a lot of work = $25,000

Seller says need to be torn down = go look at the property

In the back of this book, I have included a repair estimate sheet that you can use to better determine repairs.

DO NOT get too hung up on figuring out repairs. The best strategy is to use general estimates until you can actually go and look at the property.

Determine your Offer

The Next step is to determine what you're going offer. Generally speaking, we want to make offers anywhere from 40 to 60% of the ARV. If the house seems like it needs lots of work, you definitely want it to be lower than that.

Use the Little formula that I have provided you with. It usually comes out to pretty close to 50%

Example: ARV = $100,000 x 70% = $70,000

        Minus Repairs $15,000 (estimate) = $55,000

        Minus Closing Cost: $4,000 = $51,000

        Minus Holding Cost: $2,000 = $49,000

        Minus Selling Cost: $5,000 = $44,000

So $44,000 would be my offer on a property that is valued around $100,000.   My holding and closing cost should be around what you would normally pay, they might be a little high but better to be safe than sorry.

All of these expenses are examples and estimates; they could be higher or lower. The selling cost could be nothing but the cost of a few signs put in the front yard or they could be $5,000 for a realtor.

If you are going to wholesale the property, I would take off another $5,000 or whatever your wholesale fee is going to be.

Note: *The Reason to multiply the property by 70% is because that 30% is the rehabbers or your profit and you would always want to give rehabbers a nice profit.*

When you are planning on wholesaling or flipping the property to another investor, it is important to keep the property under 65% of the ARV. This is because lots of rehabbers use hard money lenders. Hard money lenders will not loan more than 65% of the ARV.

Making an Offer

Now you want to Call the Seller and Make your offer. If your offer is really low, be very careful not to offend the seller. Also if your offer is less than what they owe on the property, it may be a dud, or a referral.

When you call the Seller, Simply say, "Hey, this is (name) I had a chance to run some comps and I determined that I could pay $XXXX. Is that something that you could work with?"

Most sellers will not be happy with your low offer but some will say its close or yes.

If the seller says I have to think about it, just let him think and call him back in a few hours or the next day.

If the seller says we are around the same ball park, I will then set a time to go and view the property.

Written Offers

If the amount you are offering is significantly lower than what the seller is asking, then you may want to email or fax the offer.

If I am dealing with a real estate agent, I always give them a written offer.

What I do is just send a simple 1 paragraph letter, with my offer in it and a contract attached. Realtors will always ask you to fax or email them an offer, so they will have something to show to their clients.

All you need for a written offer

- Cover Letter
- Contract

After you have made your offer, you will set up a time to take a walk through the property. Make sure you give yourself around an hour to do so. I like to take my time, take pictures (Always ask the seller if it's ok), and really do a good inspection. I am also respectful of the sellers and try not to waste their time or mine.

The first inspection is mainly to give you a good overview of the property.

I always take a few contracts with me to the property, the contract is already filled out with a few different prices and I leave one of the prices blank. This way, I am ready to get the Property under contract if I feel like it's a good deal. However, there are times when I do say I will have to run some more numbers and will get back to them if the property needs lots of work.

Below is my Letter of Intent that I send to Sellers.

Letter of Intent

Dear Earl,

Thank You for giving me the opportunity to look around at your property at ▮▮▮ Stone St. From my Inspection I determined that the property needs a lot of work to bring it up to current market standards. I also ran some comparables and have based my offer on Current Market Value and the necessary repairs needed.

The Fact that the property is a 1962 Mobile makes it difficult for others to obtain financing, if we were going to resale the property we would have to carry the financing for someone. Also the fact the foundation is on rail road ties brings up more concerns and Lots of Updating is in order to bring the mobile up to Market Value.

I am offering $15,000, in as-is condition. This offer is Valid for 30 days. I am willing to purchase the property but must be able to buy it right.

Feel Free to consider this offer and talk it over with your family.

Thank you for your cooperation. I look forward to working with you.

Sincerely,

Christopher Seder

The Importance of Making Offers

One of the Biggest Reasons Investors do not Have Success

I have thought long and hard about this. I truly feel that **making offers** is the most important part of your real estate investing business. If you are not making offers, then you are not making money.

Most people wait until they find a smoking deal to make an offer. I'd say start making offers on property now. For one, it will give you some good experience and two, you might just get one. Remember to make your offer low and run it through the process above.

Make offers to realtors, for-sale by owners and everyone that has a property for sale.

This has been my biggest struggling points; I get in the funk of just looking for killer deals and do not make massive amounts of offers. I am only human.

You will not get all your offers accepted and you probably won't even get 10% of your offers accepted.

One good rule of thumb is that if you are not going to be jumping up and down after your offer is accepted, then you might have offered too much. Always think about this way. If this deal is accepted, how am I going to feel about it? If the answer is I will want to jump up and down, then you have made a good offer.

Get out there and make offers, it's the only way to get deals.

Initial Walkthrough

In this section, I am going to discuss how to do an Initial Walk through. You will be provided with an inspection check list form. The initial walkthrough is a time for you to build some rapport with the sellers. When you first meet up with the sellers, have them give you a tour of the property. You want to be making little notes throughout your walkthrough. The purpose of this walkthrough is to get a general idea of the work that needs to be done.

You want to look for any major repairs: Check all of these.

- Do the bathrooms need to be redone?
- Does the whole house need painting?
- Carpet needed?
- Kitchen Remodel?
- Ceiling
- Roof
- Siding/Exterior Paint
- Foundation/Crawlspace
- Furnace, A/C, Hot water heater

This way, you can determine if the house is going to be just some minor cosmetic repairs or a full rehab project.

Once you have determined all the repairs that need to be done, go ahead and sign a contract. If there are any major concerns, then get a professional inspector to come and look at it. I always sign the contract with a 15 day inspection contingency in my contract so I can go back and really inspect the property and have a professional look at any major concerns.

If you do not feel comfortable signing a contract until you get a professional inspections, then simply get a contractor to come over and give you an estimate of what it will cost to fix it.

Note: *The initial walkthrough is just for you to get a general idea of repairs that are needed. You can always go back and negotiate and lower the price if you find something during your inspection period.*

Inspection Form

House Address_____ Date_____

Inspection Check List	Yes	No	# Needed	Repair Cost Estimates	Repair Cost
Roof				Full Roof $8,000 - $10,000 Layer of Shingles $3,000	
Exterior Paint/ Siding				Single Family 1000-1500 sq ft $3,000 Siding $7,000 - $10,000	
Windows				$150 Apiece around $100 to install $250 - $300 a piece	
Garage Repair				Garage Door $600 Paint $500-$1000 Roof $2,000	
Yard/Land Scaping				$500 - $1000	
Heating and Furnace				Replace Furnace $1,500 Replace Hot Water Heater $500 Install Baseboard heaters $5,000	
Plumbing Repair				Plumbing (new bath, and kitchen fixtures) $2,000 per floor	
Electrical				New Panel $1,500 New Plugs and Fixtures $200 Rewire House $4,000 - $8,000	

Foundation				Reframe 1 support beam $250 Seal Basement $250 Poor Concrete $800 (3-5 years)	
Basement				Remodel and Finish : $10,000	
Interior Paint				Single Family 1500 sq ft $2,000 Larger Single Family $4,000	
Flooring Carpet/Vinyl/Tile/ Hardwood				Carpet around = $1 per sq ft $1,500 for a 1500 sq ft Padding around 65 cents per sq ft Hardwood installed = $8 per sq ft Vinyl (10x10) around $800	
Kitchen Repair				Single Family $2,000 Single Family Upgrade $4,000	
Kitchen Appliances				Fridge = $150 used $500 New Stove = $100 used $400 New Dishwasher – $300 Microwave $200	
Bathroom				Full Bath $1,500 Half Bath $1,000	
Doors				Entry Doors $150 Interior Doors $50	
Sheet Rock Damaged Sheet Rock Replaced				$3.00 per sq ft total rehab Patch work $500- $1000 Whole House $9,000 Small patches $300	
Light Fixtures				1 Fixture $10 - $50	
Decks/Porches				New Deck $2,000 Repair Deck $500	
Miscellaneous				X total by 5 to 10 %	
List Other Concerns					
				Total Repair Cost:	

You will also want to drive around the neighborhood and look at your comps before you do your initial walkthrough. That way, you can really see if your comps are truly comparable to your subject property. You will also get a good feel for the neighborhood.

Filling out the Contract

Filling out a contract can seem harder than nuclear physics to a lot of investors. But most of it is common sense. The only thing that will really vary on contracts is the purchase price, seller information, inspection period, and manner in which you are closing (cash or finance).

You want to always make the contract assignable; if you are wholesaling the property the contract must be assignable. To make the contract assignable, just put "and or assigns" after your name.

Example:

This Agreement stipulates the terms of sale of this property. Read carefully before signing. This is a legally binding contract. If not understood, seek competent advice.
_____ Billings _____ Montana, (date) _____
_____ Christopher   Seder, (and or Assigns) _____
as ☐ joint tenants with rights of a survivorship, ☐ tenants in common, ☒ single in his/her own right,

If you ever have any questions about filling a contract out, simply ask a Real estate broker to show you how to fill one out or go to a title company and have them help you. Once you have filled out one contract, you will have it down.

Always let the seller know that you will be having inspections and walking your partners through the house. You need to be able to have access to the property.

Contingencies to Add to your Contract

- Subject to Inspection and approval of partner
- Subject to property appraising for sale price – only if you are getting appraisal
- Subject to home inspection
- Subject to financing acceptable to buyer (term and rate) – if getting financing
- Buyer is a real estate investor who buys and sells property for profit
- Purchaser requests permission to have access to the property upon signing of contract, to show prospective contractors, home inspectors, business partners and Investors.
- The Buyer may assign his contract to another real estate investor who will then purchase the property.

Screen Shot from a Contract

ADDITIONAL PROVISIONS: Buyer is a Licensed Real Estate Agent is compliance with Laws of Disclosure
Buyer is a real estate investor who buys and sells property for a profit
Should buyer cancel the agreement his liability is limited to forfeture of earnest deposit
Purchaser requests permission to have access to the property upon signing of contract, to show prospective contractors, home inspectors, business partner and investors.

Contract Check list

- Buyers/Your name (and or assigns)
- Sellers Name (everyone on title)
- Price
- Inspection period (usually 15 days)
- Legal Description and Address
- Deposit (as little as possible and made payable to the title company)
- Closing Date (normally 30 days but we have closed in 3 days before)
- Signatures
- Contingencies

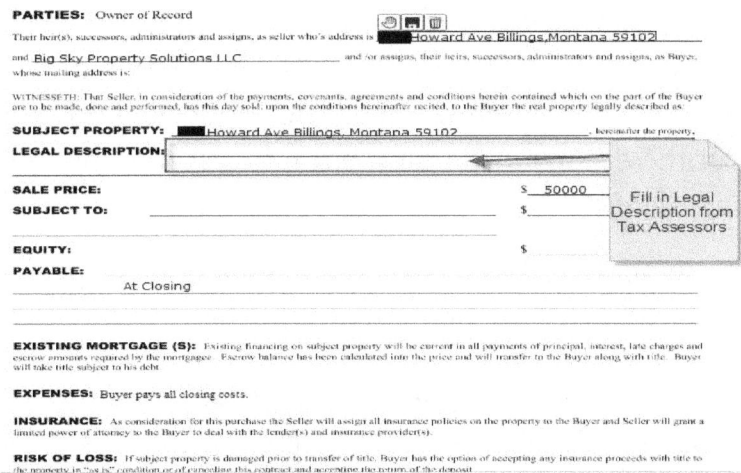

103 | P a g e

POSSESSION: Possession of the property and occupancy (tenants excepted), with all keys and garage door openers, will be delivered to the Buyer when title transfers. Leases and security deposit will transfer to the Buyer with title.

INSPECTIONS: This contract is contingent upon the Buyer's inspection and approval of the property prior to transfer of title. Seller agrees to provide access to the Buyer's representatives prior to transfer of title for inspection, repairs and to market the property.

ACCEPTANCE: This instrument will become a binding contract when accepted by the Seller and signed by both Buyer and Seller. If it is not accepted and signed by the Seller prior to 01/11/2011 , this contract shall be void.

DEPOSIT: Upon acceptance Buyer will place in escrow an earnest money deposit of 500 with American Title and Escrow which will be part of the cash paid to the Seller when title transfers. This deposit will be returned to the Buyer if title does not transfer in accordance with this agreement and said title company will close this transaction.

SELLER: Agrees that the buyer may place signs and show the property immediately upon acceptance of this contract by both parties.

CLOSING: Closing will take place on or before 01/31/2011 at American Title and Escrow . Subject to a 90 day period in which the buyer/seller shall be permitted to clear any title problems.

OTHER AGREEMENTS:

> This is where you would put any extra contingencies you want.

TIME IS OF THE ESSENCE with this agreement. Each contingency contained herein shall be satisfied according to its terms by the closing date or this contract extends to provide time for satisfaction of said contingencies. Each party shall diligently pursue the completion of this transaction. Each warranty herein made survives the closing of this transaction.

PROHIBITION: This agreement establishes a prohibition against transfer, conveyance or encumbrance to the property.

Seller	Date	Buyer _Christopher Seder_	Date 01/09/2011
Print Name		Print Name Christopher Seder Big Sky Property Solutions LLC	
Seller	Date	Buyer	Date

Formal Inspection/ your Inspection Period

Now that you have the property under contract and have decided what you are going to do with the property, you are ready to go in and do a detailed inspection of the property.   If I am wholesaling the property, I do not go to in-depth with my inspection but I do put together a rough scope of work.

You will want to know what the repairs are going to cost so you can give your buyer a good deal.

If you are wholesaling the property, this is the time that you look for a buyer. In the next chapter, I will explain how to find a buyer.

Now if you are going to rehab the property or buy the property for a rental, you are going to want to line up 3 or more contractors to give you an estimate of what they would charge to remodel the property. You can find these contacts through realtor referrals, referrals from other investors or just looking through the paper.

I will usually conduct a walkthrough on the property on my own but I use to do it with my father and he would show me what to look for. In the Rehab section, I will give you full scopes of work as examples.

If you do not know what the heck you are doing, have another investor show you how they do it or have a contractor do the walkthrough on the property with you.

What to do

Take the inspection form check list and go through every room of the house. Make notes on everything that needs to be done, room by room.

Once I have a list of everything that needs to be done, I will sit down and list out what I think each is going to cost to have it done. I have done a few rehabs and my Business partner does several a year so we know what everything is going to cost. We know that it will cost around $2,000 to get a house painted in our area.

One of the best places to find prices is at Lowes or home depot. They have a few very knowledgeable people. Bring them your list and ask if they can help price everything out for you.

Also, take your list of repairs to 3 contractors and have them go over it with you. Ask them what every little detail will cost.

Check with other investors and get estimates from them. Check with title companies to see what the pricing for a closing would be. Check with realtors for selling costs and ARV and always double check your rehab numbers with contractors.

Once you have your repairs cost, insert it in a formula to check your numbers and make sure the deal will work. You might want to even add 10% to make sure you have not left off any minor repairs.

Double Check Your Numbers

After Repair Value

- Rehab Costs
- Closing Cost
- Carrying Costs
- <u>Selling Costs</u>

= Profit

Note: *I will provide you with a sample scope of work and inspection check list.*

Steps in Evaluating Deals

1. Lead Sheet Interview
2. Property Card – County Assessor's office
3. Comparable Property – Print out
4. Determine your Offer Price
5. Make your Offer
6. Drive the Neighborhood
7. Initial Walk Through
8. Negotiating with Seller
9. Sign Contract
10. Walk through again
11. Put scope of work together
12. Close on the Property or Wholesale (Closing and Wholesaling are coming in the Next Chapter's)

Chapter 5

Getting Your House SOLD!

The Art of Wholesaling!

"Think of yourself as on the threshold of unparalleled success. A whole, clear, glorious life lies before you. Achieve! Achieve!"

-Andrew Carnegie

At this point, you should know what you are doing with your house, you have figured out your exit strategy or have a few in mind. You should have your contract signed a 15 day inspection period and closing in 30 days or whatever is in your contract.

In this section, I am going to talk about:

- How to find wholesale buyers.
- Wholesaling Your House

If you are planning on doing any other strategies, there are several other courses on them. Check out **ChristopherSeder.**com for more info on other courses. They are a little more complicated and it would take another book to explain.

Wholesaling Your House

When wholesaling a property, you get the property under contract and then simply assign your contract to another investor buyer. You collect an assignment fee and move on to another deal.

Remember that you are not actually buying the property when wholesaling. Sometimes you will close on a property. For example, your buyer needs to close today and you know it's a great deal. So you close on the property and then might wholesale it to another investor. If you are going to wholesale a bank owned property you will have to close on it. (but you can flip in right away and still make a lot of $$$)

Finding Wholesale Buyers

Your Goal should be to have a HUGE buyers list. Every time you have a wholesale deal, investors should be calling you like crazy. Once you have established that you provide real estate investors with amazing deals, you will not have to work hard to find a buyer.

With a big buyers list, you can just email your list saying you have a new deal and wait for the phone to ring. You should start building your buyers list before you ever have a real estate deal but it's not required because if you have a deal, you will find a buyer. The main reason I say start building your buyers list first is because it's good to know what type of deals other investors are looking for and what they are paying.

Building Your Buyers List

Building Your Buyers List can be one of the easiest things. I think it is one of the easiest parts of your real estate investing Business. I have heard lots of people saying that it's hard but believe me if you have good deals, Buyers will be tracking you down.

To run a successful wholesaling business, you will need to have cash buyers. If you have 5 good wholesale buyers who pay all cash and can close quickly, you can make tons of money wholesaling.

So who are your buyers? Other Investors, Rehabbers, Landlords, and anyone who wants to pay all cash for a house. Now that you know who you are looking for where, do you think these people would hang out?

Your Local REIA

The First Place to look is at your Local Real Estate Investors Association. Most cities and towns have one and they usually meet once a month. You can Google Your Area and REIA to find one. You can also go to http://www.nationalreia.com/

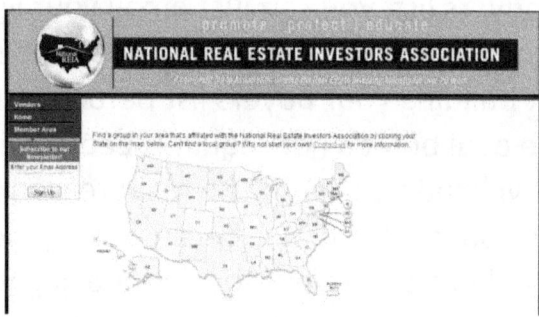

The REIA is a Great Place to start building your buyers list; you will have all kinds of investors at the REIA. Make Sure You Bring Your Business Cards and Hand them Out to Everyone. Get everyone's cards and tell them you are finding tons of cheap houses right now. Ask them if they would be interested in being added to your buyers list.

Become Best friends with the President of the REIA, they have the list and names of all the members. You could have the President Blast your Deals out to hundreds or thousands of investors. Think About it.

I have always asked investors what type of houses they are looking for, areas, and what the maximum price they will pay. Most of them will usually tell me anything if it's a deal. Try and get more specific with them, and say ok if I bring you anything that is a deal and will you buy it? And maybe they will then get a little more specific.

If you can really narrow down what investors are looking for, it will help you figure out what kinds of houses to put under contract.

The Court House Steps

The next place to find Buyers is Foreclosure auctions. When buying properties at foreclosure auction, you are required to have a cashier's check or proof of funds. What that means is that anyone bidding on property at the auction has cash to buy properties.

Investors at these auctions are looking to buy cheap property and make money. After the Auction or prior to the auction, talk to these people and tell them you are a wholesaler and ask if they would be interested in Cheap Properties.

Run Classified Ads

I usually post a classified ad every day or so on Craigslist.org. You can find some of my classified ad examples in the Classified Ad riches eBook.

I seem to get a buyer or two to join every time I post an ad.

Freedomsoft

Freedomsoft-4.com has a section where you can pull all of the cash buyers for your area. They compile data from recent houses that have sold for all cash. All you have to do is hit the search button and BOOM, you instantly have cash buyers. You can then contact these people to buy your house. Go to **http://freedomsoft-4.com** for more info.

The Realtor's MLS

You can find cash buyers on the MLS. It's pretty simple to do but you do need to have MLS access. If you're a licensed realtor, you can do this easily. If not, have realtors do it for you.

- Simply do a quick search on the MLS

- Go to status, Sold/Closed and Enter Your Zip Code or City
- Go to Add more Search Criteria and look for Sold Terms, this will allow you to find all the houses that were sold in CA$H.
- Then Simply Hit Submit
- They Are All Your Cash Buyers.
- You will Also Have to Cross Reference the Property with the County Records, to find the actual name of the Owner.

Once you have the owners' names, you can send them a letter telling them about you and how you can provide them with cheap property.

It's pretty simple and I hope that all made since to you.

To Recap here are some ways to find your buyers

1. REIA Meetings
2. Foreclosure Auctions
3. Classified Ads
4. List Source/Public Records
5. MLS

Wholesaling a House with no Buyers List

What if you do not have a list right now but you have a wholesale deal? Here are a few things that you can do to find wholesale buyer leads and sell your house.

1. Put out bandit signs (not in the front yard)

Put bandit signs all over the neighborhood and at all the major stop signs near the property. Do not put the address, just put "cheap house for sale" "Fixer Upper" "Wholesale Property" or something like that and your phone number.

2. Put an Ad Up on Craigslist and Back Page

You can make simple little professional looking flyers that can be put up on craigslist on a site called V-Flyer. Check it out.

3. Run an Ad in your local Paper
4. Put your Ad on Other Sites Like (Zillow.com, Truila.com, Cyberhomes.com, Homes.com)
5. Put your House on Your Blog and Web Site
6. Take your Deal to Your Local Real Estate Club President

Every city or most have a local real estate investing association and the president of that club has a buyers list of hundreds or thousands.   Find the REIA nearest you and call the president. Tell them you have a killer deal and was wondering if they knew of any members looking for what you have.

Now you will have buyers contacting you like crazy. Remember we are just putting a motivated seller together with a motivated buyer.

You are going to get several different types of buyers calling you.

- Some will just ask you for the address and say thanks.
- Some will ask you tons of questions.
- Some will want to see the inside of the property and want to set up a time to meet with you.
- Other buyers will make you an offer right there and then.

One thing to remember is that if we are wholesaling the property, it's going to be hard to walk tons of buyers through the house. We should have told the seller and put in a contingency that we are able to walk inspectors and partners through the property.

If you have several people that want to see the property before they make an offer, we need to pre-screen them first.

The best way to pre-screen is to tell them this is a cash sale or hard money sell only and ask if they could email or fax you their proof of funds. Some buyers will not like this.

Once you have found a few cash buyers that are interested, call up your seller and set up a time to walk them through the house.

Before you go to the property with your buyer, tell them that you have the property under contract right now and that they need to present themselves as either one of your partners or inspectors. If they deviate from this plan, we will not be able to do business anymore.

We want the buyers who make offers right away

To determine if we are talking to good Wholesale Buyers, we have to evaluate our buyer. Making sure your wholesale buyer is serious and this is why pre-screening them is very important. You will waste lots of valuable time messing around with unqualified buyers.

When you first meet or talk with a buyer, you want to gather as much information as you can. You need to make sure your buyer actually has the money to buy your wholesale property. Ask how they close on property. Do they use Cash, Hard Money, Financing, or Private Money? You also need to know how fast they can close on a property. Do not always take the buyers word that they can pay all cash. Ask if they can get you a proof of funds from their bank, I let them know that I will require one.

Another good thing to know is how experienced they are. Experienced investors can really make the process run smoothly.

How to Choose Between Multiple Offers

Cash is the business we want to be in because it makes deals easier to close and go faster. If I am choosing between different offers on a property, I will always look for offers that are all cash terms first. If you go with someone looking to finance the property, you will spend countless of weeks with the seller calling you asking when you are going to close and you having to chase the buyer around asking them. It will become a mess. If you can avoid it, only deal with cash buyers.

Just use your judgment to determine which offer you want to accept. Look for closing date (how fast they can close), terms, and pick one you like best.

Assign the Contract

After you choose your offer, simply fill out an assignment contract with your buyer. Take the contract and assignment to the title company or your closing attorney and your job is done.   Just tell the title company to start the title process.

Agreement to Assign Contract for Sale and Purchase

Subject Property: Howard Ave, Billings MT, 59102.
Legal Description: (copy from Contract)

This agreement is made between Big Sky Property Solutions LLC. (ASSIGNOR) and (Your End Buyer) (ASSIGNEE) regarding purchase of above referenced SUBJECT PROPERTY.

Whereas Big Sky Property Solutions LLC (BUYER) has entered into a Purchase and Sales Agreement with (SELLER) for the purchase of SUBJECT PROPERTY, and whereas BUYER wishes to assign its rights, interests and obligations in the Purchase and Sales Agreement, it is hereby agreed between ASSIGNOR and ASSIGNEE as follows:
1.   ASSIGNEE shall pay ASSIGNOR a NON-REFUNDABLE assignment fee Of (Your Assignment Fee).
2.   Assignee's inspection period shall expire upon execution of this Assignment. ASSIGNEE accepts all terms and conditions of the contract for Sale and Purchase between BUYER and SELLER in its entirety.
3.   ASSIGNEE acknowledges receipt of legible copies of the original Contract for Sale and Purchase in its entirety including all Addendums associated with this transaction.
4.   Additional terms and conditions of this Assignment are as follows:
     -   This assignment contract is non-assignable without the express written consent of the ASSIGNOR.
     -   No changes to the Purchase Contract can be made without written Consent of (Your Name)
5.   Disclosures and Acknowledgement:
     a) ASSIGNOR and affiliated associates make no warranty, expressed or implied, regarding inspection reports or other reports provided to ASSIGNEE by ASSIGNOR or third parties concerning this property.
     b) ASSIGNEE acknowledges they are conducting a transaction dealing directly with ASSIGNOR for the purchase of SUBJECT PROPERTY. ASSIGNEE is not relying upon or being represented by a REAL ESTATE BROKERAGE in this transaction.

AGREED AND ACCEPTED

ASSIGNOR (_____)   ASSIGNOR (_____)

Chapter 6

Closing on Your Deal

Yes, This is where you get Your CA$H

"Owning a home is a keystone of wealth - both financial affluence and emotional security"

-Suzie Orman

The closing process is not a very complicated process if you are working with a great title company or closing attorney. Ask other experienced investors who they use for closing and ask your Local real estate investors association who they use. Our real estate investors association BigSKYREIA.com gets a members discount at certain title companies. Check with the reia to see if they have a title company that will give investor discounts.

Let's Start off with talking about a Wholesale Close

Someone wants to buy your wholesale deal? Awesome. So you go through and qualify them, make sure they have cash to close the transaction and go over their offer.

The next step is to get the Buyer to Sign an Agreement to assign contract. In this agreement, you are just assigning your rights and responsibilities to buy the property to your investor buyer.

When assigning a Contract you must also get a deposit from your buyer. They can make it payable to you or to the title company. The deposit from your buyer should be more than the deposit you gave to your seller. This way if the deal falls through, you will still make a little profit from their deposit.

I recommend that you get a non-refundable deposit from your buyer. By doing this, you can make sure they are serious. No buyer will give you a non-refundable deposit unless they are positive that they will close. Some buyers will not want to give you one and that's ok, a non-refundable one just makes your life easier.

Ok so once you have your contract with the buyer all filled out, you just fax everything over to the title company or take it there. Say to them "I have a new deal, please start a title search and advice". Give them your contact info and the information for the buyer and seller.

Most title companies will handle all the details involved in the closing process. Always tell the title company to contact the buyers or sellers directly if they have any questions for them.

Now your job is done and everything is out of your hands. That was pretty simple wasn't it? All that's left is for the title company to coordinate the closing and them to call you when you check it ready.

Sometimes you will want to follow up with your buyer and seller to make sure everyone is happy. You can also attend the closing if you would like or just wait for your check.

Closing on the property when you are the Buyer

You have gone through the process of evaluating the property, signed a contract, completed an inspection and determined that you are going to buy the property.   You will want to fax your title company your contract and tell them to start the title process.

Here is the Closing Process if you are getting a loan
   (starts after you get property under contract)

1. Schedule the Home Inspection
2. Lender will order Preliminary Title Report
3. Check with City Building Inspector to Make sure there are no code violations
4. Lender will be processing your loan
5. They will also order an appraisal
6. After Loan is approved, Inspection ok, appraisal ok, and title clear.
7. Schedule closing with title company
      i. They will order any loan pay offs
      ii.   And Gather all lenders required loan documents put the closing package together. They will meet with both the buyer and seller to sign and notarize all documents. They will record all necessary documents at the clerk and recorder's office and pay off any mortgage on the property and disburse all funds.

As you can see, it's pretty simple. The title company pretty much does everything for you. If you are paying all cash, the process is a little different but not much. You could just take everything involving the lender and you simply open up escrow with the title and they will handle everything.

Funding Options

There are several different ways to fund your real estate investment. You can use Bank Financing, All Cash, a Hard Money Lender, your IRA, 1031 Exchanges or Owner Financing. All of them can be great options. You should research all of the different methods and learn how to use all of them effectively.

We use traditional bank financing on a lot of our rental property and owner financing. It's great because you buy the property and have your renters paying down the mortgage and giving you monthly cash flow. The down side with traditional bank financing is that the criteria for getting a loan are getting ridiculous. You have to have an amazing credit, 20% down and dance like a monkey. Most people are just getting started cannot afford it.

We try to get owner financing whenever possible. You can get great interest rates from owners and give them some monthly cash flow.

Another Option is Hard Money Lenders. Hard money lenders will lend you 60-65% of the After Repair Value and Charge you 3-5 points (1 point =1% of what you are loaning) plus 12-15% interest. They will also loan you the money to repair your property. I know several people who use them and love them. You can get quick cash to fund all of your rehab property. Only use Hard Money lenders on real estate flips. If you're paying 15% interest for too long, it could break you.

My Favorite Method is "All Cash", the reason I like all cash is because it's easy and quick. You might be saying but I do not have that much money? Well, you can get the cash from private money lenders, a line of credit on your personal house or even a line of credit from your whole life insurance policy.

One of your goals should be to find a good private money lender to work with. With this, you can have cash you need to close on deals with in just a matter of days, instead of the weeks or months it takes to get bank financing approved.

Finding Private Money to Fund Your Deals

A huge hurdle to getting into real estate is money. Everyone thinks that you have to have tons of cash to

 become a real estate investor but that is not true. If you can find private money lenders to fund all your deals, you will never have to put up a cent. Remember this material is in my view and always consult a licensed attorney before going ahead with anything I say.

What are the benefits of using private money?

- No Banks, which means no credit checks
- Better terms
- Speed of Funds
- No application process
- 100% financing
- Everything is Negotiable

Finding private money is not as hard as you think. You just have to have some Balls and get out of your comfort zone until you become big time. Private money lenders are not going to be knocking on your door giving you money but when you become successful, people will be lining up to lend you their money.

Before we even talk about where to find private money lenders, I want to tell you that you need to set up some kind of credibility pack.   The packet should have things like.

- Company Summary
- Case Studies of Rehab Projects or Deals You have done
    - If you have not done any deals then Fake it till you make it, don't lie just give an example.
    - You need something to show candidates what you do.
- Your Investor Program and Descriptions
- FAQ
- Forms - Promissory Note, Mortgage deed, deed of trust, Etc.
- Business Cards

I know you may be lost right now but having some kind of packet and pitch always ready is important. You can also make a cool power point presentation to give to potential lenders.

Where do you find Private Money Lenders?

Anywhere and Everywhere. Just think about it. Do you know anyone who might be rich? A Doctor? Lawyer? Simply bring these people out to lunch and always pay for their meals. Ask them if they would like to get a better return on their money than what they are getting in the stock market. Give them a little pitch. Like I have said before, you are going to have to step out of your comfort zone and do something.

Tell these people they can use their whole life insurance policy, IRA's, Cash or even credit. Let them know that you can give them a way better return on their money than any other investments.

Other Places to find Private Money Lenders

- o Your Buyers List, There are other Investors Who Have Cash on Hand
- o Friends and Family
- o Busy Professionals
- o Through Attorneys
- o Through Accountants
- o Business Networking Event
- o Chamber Events
- o Freedomsoft-4.com (private lender database)

You want to be educating these people about investing with you. Below is a little section out of my Investment Program. Give these people a little pitch like, "Hey, would you be interested in earning a guaranteed 8-12% return on your money backed by real estate?" They Say,

"Of Course!" You, "Here is my Card. Let's set up a time for me to show you what I do".

Then you sit down with them and go through your credibility pack with them. You can use the examples below as part of your investment program pack.

Investment Programs

We buy and sell houses. To buy the houses, we prefer to borrow money from private individuals who we pay 8-12% to use your money. It is a really simple plan.

What we do is to locate a property that we want to buy. We buy properties anywhere from 30 to 50% of the ARV.

Then we borrow from you to purchase the property. We have a formal closing and you get a mortgage on the home with other documents. You get a promissory note, mortgage deed or deed of trust, hazard insurance policy, personal guarantee, title insurance and appraisal.

- 8-12% Annual Simple interest rate

- 6-12 Month Terms

- Principle and interest payable at the sale

- Secured by subject property

- Lender gets the mortgage deed or deed of trust, to protect their interest

    o We cannot sell without your approval

An Example:

$100,000 Purchase price

$30,000 Rehab

ARV of 200K and as is value of 150K

Loan to ARV 65%

Investor lending 100% = $130,000 at 12%

6 Month payable upon re-sale   130,000 x .12 x 6/12 = $7,800

Seven Day Funding Example, this is a Wholesale Transaction Funding

$100,000 Purchase Price

Investor Lending 100k at 12% or 1-2 points guaranteed

7 day flip 100k x .12 x 7/365 = $230.14

Or 1 point which guarantees $1,000 for seven days of money use, not bad for 7 days.

So the process is pretty simple. Remember to talk to an attorney and get all the proper documents before you proceed and just make sure you are not breaking any SEO rules with lending money.

So get out there and find private money. Get aggressive and get out of your comfort zone.

Action Plan:

- Get out and start telling people about your business

- Think of all of the successful people you might know

  - Take them to lunch and tell them about the business you are getting into.

- Contact your Local REIA and find out who they use for a title company or closing attorney.

Chapter 7

Flip that House

This is where the Big MONEY is Made

You might know this process from TV shows like flip this house. The investor buys an ugly rundown property and fixes it up. The house is then sold to a buyer looking to live in the home.   The investor collects and huge check and life is good.

If you choose to fix up your property and re-sell the property or keep it as a rental, this section is for you. Wholesaling is a way to make a quick profit, usually an average of $3,000 to $10,000.   Rehabbing is a way to make an average of $30,000 or more.   Do four rehabs a year and you have made over $100,000.

In order to be an effective wholesaler, you must also know the rehabbing process. You need to know what it's actually going to take to fix up a property. We want to help our wholesale buyers as much as possible and give them good deals. After you have some cash and experience from wholesaling, rehabbing is the next step.

It is important to educate yourself on the rehabbing process because you need to know what material costs and how much labor will cost. A good rehab knows how to handle contractors and manage a project. Once you can master all of that, you will then be a real dangerous rehabber. You do not need to master everything before doing a rehab, just know the basics and learn as you go.

Rehab Overview

It's best to break the rehab process down into several small steps.   It can be very complicated if everything is jumbled up together. If you know where to start and where to finish, it will help you out a lot.

I am starting at the walkthrough phase; since we covered it a little in the wholesaling section, I will not go too in-depth. This is the walkthrough during your inspection period.

You need to go through the property and really get a good list of what needs to be done. Some people choose to do this after they have closed the property and sometimes you might have to but I like to do it before, so I know what's going on. If I find any major concerns, I can get a professional to look at it.

The process before the initial walkthrough is exactly the same as the wholesaling process. I Will Skip the actual Closing on the house with the seller but there is a section in this book dedicated to closing on property.

Walkthrough Inspection

The walk through inspection is very important. This is where you will really know if this is going to be a deal that you want to go ahead and do or cancel the contract. When I walk through the property, I make sure I have a Few tools.

- Camera
- Property Inspection Form
- Notebook
- Keys (if can get from homeowner)
- Flashlight

- Lockbox (if you have already purchased put on lock box)

The Purpose of this walkthrough is to really get a good Idea of everything that needs to be done. Use my inspection form; it will give you a good Idea. What you have to do is look at everything in detail and check what needs to be done and what does not.

I also like to take a note book with me and go through room by room. I then write everything that needs to be done in each room. Below is an example of Part of what I do for a scope of work

Scope of Work Room by Room

Exterior	Yes	No	What to Repair
Siding			
Roof			
Windows			
Paint			
Gutters			
Lights			
Door			
Yard			
Other			

What to Do.

1. Fill out the Inspection form
2. List out Room by Room
3. Pictures

That's really all you need to do. The inspection form is pretty easy to use.

Scope of Work

Once you get back home or to your office, you will need to put all of your findings into a scope of work and material list. A scope of work is simply an itemized list of everything that needs to be done.

Example: Have a Section that says Exterior, Break that down into Siding, Paint, Trim, Gutters, or whatever needs to be done on the exterior. All the Materials needed Should Be broken down.

Exterior	Yes	No	What to Repair
Siding			
Roof			
Windows			
Paint			
Gutters			
Lights			
Door			
Yard			
Other			

If you are not experienced with what materials you will need for certain jobs, you will need to ask someone. Go to Lowes with a list of everything that needs to be done and price it all out. We have done enough rehabs where we know what and how much materials we are going to need and what it will cost.

Once you gain experience, you can just use scope of works from past jobs and your knowledge.

You Give the Blank scope of works to your contractors who will then give you price estimates on everything that needs to be done.

Example Broken down Scope of Work (from trailer)

	Quantity	Material	labor	Total
Carpet	534 sq ft	$539.58	$97	
Pad		$256.32		
Carpet Edging Trim		$18.42		
Paint Brushes	1 Pack	$11.00		
Rollers		$3.50		
Masking Tape	2 Rolls	$8.94		
Paint	2 Gallons	$29.94		
Kilz	1 Gallon	$14.97		
Drop Cloths	3	$8.50		
Light Bulbs	2 Packs	$3.00		
Roof Coating	5 Gallons	$70.00		
Door Trim	5 Pieces	$21.40		
Range Hood	1	$40		
Stove	1	$100		
Fridge	1	$130		
Light Fixtures	3	$45		
Doors	2	$60		
Mini Blinds	13	$80		
Kitchen Trim	50 ft	$30		
Plywood		$50		
Closet Glass Door	1	$77		
Other Items		$200		
Bathroom Floor Remodel and Handyman work	1 Day Work		$200	
Total		$1,527.57	$297	$1,824.57

Example of Scope of Work (note it's not broken down)

	Material	Labor	Total
Demo	$400	$600	$1,000
Exterior	$154	$2000	$2,154
Electrical	$500	$600	$1,100
Sheet Rock	$50	$800	$850
Painting Interior	$180	$1500	$1680
Window	$2000	$500	$2,500
Bathrooms	$1125	$720	$1,845
Flooring	$2000	$0	$2,00
Kitchen	$1100	$1000	$2,100
Appliances	$1300	$0	$1,300
Land Scaping	$200	$500	$700
TOTAL	**$9,009**	**$8,220**	**$17,229**

Contractors and Job Bidding

I had touched on having contractors bid on your jobs a little earlier. What I do is to make a several blank copies of my scope of work. I will then Leave the Scopes of work at the property or Give them to my Contractors Directly. My Contractors can then see what I want to be done in detail and only give me estimates on my needs.

Make sure you inform your contracts to give detailed estimates. You want to know what the contractors are charging you for. I want to know if they are charging me $500 to screw in a light bulb.

Always get 3 or more contractors to bid on your job. When you have three or more scopes of work to compare, you can then really see which contractors are trying to charge you more and which are the most competitive. Some contractors may charge more of certain tasks.

Do not always go with the cheapest contractors because they might not be the best at times. Just find a contractor that you feel will do a good job at a reasonable price. You can always negotiate for a better price with them if you feel their price is too high.

Always make sure the contractors you are using are licensed, certified and have errors and emissions insurance. You could get into lots of trouble if they do not have insurance. If something were to happen on your job, you could get sued.

Signing Contractors

Once you have had time to evaluate all of the contractors' quotes, make your decision on who is going to help you fix up your rehab. It's not time to sit down with the contractor and fill out some paper work.

Documents you need to get filled out.

1. Independent Contractor Agreement
2. Scope of work – Any Changes you came up with
3. Payment Schedule- Never Pay everything upfront. Pay when certain Mile Stones are reached. Break it down into 4 or 5 payments and pay the bulk of it when the job is done.
4. Contractor Insurance Indemnification Form
5. W9 Tax Form

6. Final and Unconditional Wavier of Lien- does not need to be signed until job is complete but good to make sure they will sign one, when the job is complete. Ask them upfront.

All of these documents above must be signed and saved by you.

For your first few jobs, make sure that you buy all the materials. Just sit down with your contractor and have them list out with you everything that you will need. This way, you will know that they are not charging you more for the materials.

Once you have established some sort of trust with your contractors or a contractor, you can then have them start buying materials for you.

Pull your Permits

Once you close on the property, you should have your contractor submit any permits that are needed. Your job could be shut down for weeks if you do not have the correct permits pulled.   Check with your City to make sure you have the right permits.   Always, Always, Always get permits and make sure your contractor pulls them.

Before you close on the property, the title company should have run a title search and checked for any liens on the property. Sometimes, the city will have a lien on the property and if there was one, the title company should have found it before you closed on the property.

However, if the lien is not on record, the title company will not find the lien.

What can you do about this?

Go to the Building Department and Pull all permits. You will also want to check if there are any building violations on the property.   Find out what the city requires to fix any violations.

Next you will want to check the city planning department for zoning changes and issues. Determine if there are any changes that could affect the value of your property.

The city code enforcement office is a place where you can check to see if there are any active code violations on the property. If there is, you will need to get the seller to get them fixed or do them yourself. It's no big deal if the violation is only cosmetic and can be fixed through your rehab process.

The title company should check the clerk and recorders for you to see if there are any other active violations. Once you are all clear, you can close on the property and start you rehab.

Rehabbing Process

You are probably thinking that, "Wow! There is a lot that I need to do before I even get started fixing up a house". You are right. It will be hard to be successful in this business if you do not prepare and do your homework before you start. You need to make every effort in protecting yourself first and take out a lot of the risk.

1. **Demo and Clean out**
This part is pretty self-explanatory. You are just getting all the junk out, tearing out the carpets and removing anything that is not staying in the house.

2. **Frame- out**
If you are doing any kind of carpentry work or framing, this is the time to do it.

3. **Rough-out**
Electrical, plumbing, heating, cooling, and duck works, etc

4. **Inspection –**
Do or have an inspection done by a head contractor to make sure everything has been done.   You may be required to have city property inspector inspect your property.

5. **Insulation**

6. **Finishing**
You can now sheet rock, tape, sand, trim out doorways, windows. You are then ready to paint and lastly, lay out the carpet.

7. **Final Touches**
Clean up the house and then stage the house so it can be sold.

Note: *This is just an example of the process and not a detailed description.*

Job Completion

Now that the job is done and satisfied with everything, you can pay your contractors and have them sign a lien release form.

Sell that House

Now that you have your property all fixed up and ready to go, how are you going to sell your house? You can either sell your property by owner or use a Real Estate Agent.

When selling by owner, you do a lot of the same marketing strategies you used to find motivated sellers. Put your property online, post classified ads; put your property on online house listing directories, bandit signs around the area, flyers, and yard signs. You want to get the word out to everyone that you have an amazing house you are looking to sell.

You can also hold an open house. Open houses are great ways to find buyers, and you may find buyers for your next fix and flip.

The only problem with selling yourself is that it can be very time consuming. It could also take longer if you do not get the message out everywhere.

A Real Estate Agent can be a great option for you to retail your property. An agent can free up your time so you can be out looking for more real estate deals.   The best thing about an agent is that they have access and can post your property on the MLS. This service goes out to thousands of agents who all have lists of retail buyers.

The only problem with a real estate agent is the 6% commission but if you have lots of profit in your deal why not just get a real estate agent to do all the selling for you and manage the closing process.

Action Steps:

- Contact 3 to 5 contractors in your area. Tell them about your business and have them bid your next wholesale deal or rehab project.

- Start compiling a data base of good contractors

Chapter 8

Deals Step By Step

In this chapter I want to give you a few steps to have success in real estate investing. The overview process for wholesaling, rehabbing, and renting a house is all lined out for you.

Wholesaling

1. Find the Property
2. Get the Property Under Contract
3. Call Potential Buyers
4. Assign the Contract and Collect deposit from Buyer
5. Take the Contract and Assignment to the Title Company
6. Attend the Closing
7. Collect your Assignment Fee

Rehabbing

1. Find the Property
2. Get House under Contract
3. Do Your Inspection
4. Line up Contractors
5. Close on the Property
6. Rehab the House
7. Final Clean up
8. Stage the House
9. List with realtor or on Own
10. Hold an Open house
11. Sell the House
12. Collect Your Check

Renting

1. Find Property
2. Put house under contract
3. Do inspection
4. Line up contractors
5. Close on the property
6. Rehab
7. Clean Up
8. List your House for rent on Craigslist
9. Run background check on tenants
10. Pick a Good Tenant
11. Collect Your Rent Checks

As you can see, the Steps <u>are</u> pretty easy in Each Deal and you should have no problem working your way through a deal.

Chapter 9

Case Studies
Learn from Our
Experience

I feel that showing you actual deals that have been done and what you will make on your investment is a great way for you to learn.

When I firstly started, I never thought I would write a book so I never thought about taking before and after pictures. Now because everyone loves to see before and after pictures I try and take them when I remember.

Just imagine if my father had put all of his flips together, he could have a book with 1200 transactions in it. That is a massive amount of pictures.

These case studies should give you a good understanding of some of the ways we buy houses and how you can make great money flipping houses, renting houses and several creative financing techniques.

Wholesaling case studies!

How to make $1,961.25 per hour

I want to tell you a little story about a recent wholesale deal I completed. This Deal took me a total of around 4 HOURS to complete. Yes 4 hours of work.

Let's start from the beginning........

A few weeks ago I was driving around a few neighborhoods. Looking for Vacant Houses, and looking for fixer uppers.   This day I had compiled a list of about 50 or so vacant houses that I would sent a Letter too.

Over the next few days I had sent out several letters and my phone rang like crazy. One call was from a lady who had a rental property that she said was a DUMP!.

Over the phone I negotiated with her (she was a tough negotiator).   But we finally settled on a price of $55,000

CA$H. Which I though was fair, I ran comparable sales on the property and fixed up it would be worth around $140,000.

The seller's husband who was on title was out of the country but she gave me his email and I sent him a contract for $55,000. The next day he emailed me back a signed contract. I had a deal.............

I then went and looked at the property, my over the phone estimate of about 25,000 to 30,000 in repairs was spot on.....

I then called an investor (cash buyer), who came over and looked at the property. I offered the property to him for $63,000, he said he would take and the next day I had him sign an assignment of contract for $8,000.

I took the contract and the assignment to the title company and my work was pretty much done. The title company then handled all of the closing and sent me a check. One small thing that the title company had to do was to get the Seller (who was out of the country), to go to the US embassy and have all of the closing documents notarized (I paid for this for the seller; I know I am a nice guy). Once all of that was complete, which only took 1 week. The property ended up closing in less than 3 weeks after I put the house under contract.

As you can see I really did not do a lot of work and cashed a Check for $7,345.26 plus a $500 earnest money deposit paid by the buyer

This all started with my going out and finding a Vacant House........... **http://VacantHouseRiches.net**

The Buy and Hold Wholesale Deal!

The next wholesale deal I want to talk to you about is a property we actually purchased with the intent of rehabbing and making a large amount of cash on. This

property was located in a small little resort town. My wife found this property while we were staying over the weekend in the town. The property was listed by a realtor and seemed like a perfect fixer upper. The property was listed for $90,000 with an arv when fixed up of around $150,000. The property needed around $30,000 to $40,000 in work.

On Monday the following week I ended up sending the realtor an offer on the property at $45,000. We ended up settling on $60,000 cash. This would give us around $50,000 in profit after we fixed up the property.

We ended up purchasing the property and started getting very busy on other projects. Because this property was over an hour away from us it sat for a couple months. I ended up putting a small yellow sign that read "Cheap House for Sale" and my phone number. I mainly just put this sign up in case something happened to the house someone would have a phone number to call. Well little did I know I started getting several calls? I ended up finding a buyer who was looking for a vacation home that was a fixer upper (he was a contractor).

We ended up selling the property to this guy for $80,000. $20,000 over what we had paid for it. After holding and closing cost we ended up making somewhere around $17,000 on the property. Not to bad for buying a house and doing nothing with it.

AMERICAN TITLE & ESCROW OF CARBON COUNTY
SHORT TERM ESCROW ACCOUNT
PO BOX 10
RED LODGE, MT 59068

FIRST INTERSTATE BANK
RED LODGE, MT 59068
93-168/929

Escrow No.: 10-

PAY   SEVENTY SEVEN THOUSAND ONE HUNDRED FOURTEEN AND 36/100 DOLLARS
TO THE
ORDER OF

DATE   1/28/2013   AMOUNT   77,114.36

Big Sky Property Solutions LLC
P.O. Box 475

Hardin, MT 59034

Wholesale Deal Listed by a realtor

This Wholesale deal was listed by a realtor for $60,000. The house needed around $20,000 in work and was worth around $100,000.

I put the property under contract for $40,000 by making an all cash offer. There was another offer that was higher but my offer was fast cash so the seller took the property.

All I did was send out 3 emails to my list of buyers, posted a few craigslist adds and had buyers flocking to me trying to get this deal. We assigned the contract to a guy looking for a rental. He gave us a $2,000 deposit and paid $3,500 to us a few days before closing.

We made $5,000 in less than 1 week and I only looked at the property after the house was assigned. Yes, I flipped this house without seeing the property first.

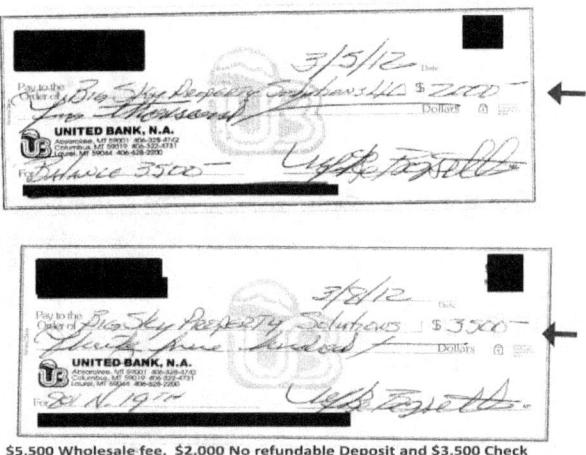

$5,500 Wholesale fee, $2,000 No refundable Deposit and $3,500 Check

Fix and Flip Case Study

This property was listed by a realtor for $145,000. Based on the repairs needed and the After Repair Value, we offered $100,000 and our offer was accepted.

We put around $22,000 into the property. (Paint, carpet, appliances, finished basement, installed basement bathroom, fixtures and so on)

Before we were even done rehabbing the property, we had several buyers making offers on the property. We listed the property for $159,900 and it was sold right away.

Total Investment $122,000. Sold for $159,900 we paid around $4,000 in closing costs. After everything was said and done, we made around $33,000.

Not too shabby for a rehab Project.

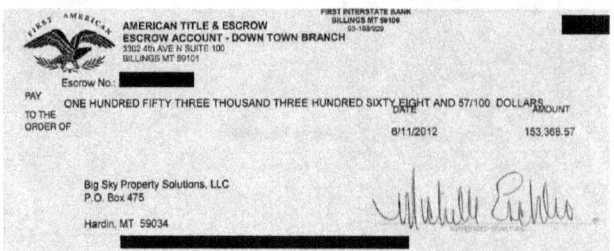

Busy Street Fix and Flip Case Study

This fix and flip property was one we found while browsing craigslist. The seller said something like come and buy my house from me before the bank takes it.

Talk about motivated.

My Father went and sat with the seller for over 2 hours talking with him before finally getting this property under contract. What we did was take the property over subject to the existing mortgage of $95,000. We brought the sellers loan current (he was behind $9,000) and also paid the seller $6,000 to walk away.

This property took us around 2 months to rehab a then another 5 months to find a buyer. But we ended up closing the property and walking away with $22,000 in profit.

Purchase Price of $110,000
Rehab Cost of $25,000
Sold for $169,000

After closing, holding and paying the buyers closing cost we made $22,000.

(Check from the case busy street fix and flip)

Small Town MT Fix and Flip Project

Here is a Rehab that we completed. These pictures are from a few months after the rehab was completed and sellers have been in the house for a while now. This house was closed on with a line of credit.

Purchased for $25,000
Rehab Cost $8,000
Total Cost $33,000

Sold for $67,500

Closing Costs	
Paid Sellers Closing Cost	$2,500
Title Insurance	$450
Deed Prep	$100
Closing fee	$200
Total Closing	**$3,250**
After Closing	**$64,250**

$64,250 - $33,000 = $31,250 in Profit

The house took around 120 days to complete, from buying, rehabbing to selling. The house could have been sold quicker but it took around 60 days for all of the end buyers financing to come together.

Just a Quick Paid Job Fix and Flip

Purchased for $87,000
Rehab Cost $1,000
(Carpet Shampoo, Lawn Mowed, Inside Painted)

Sold for $119,900

Closing Cost	
Title Ins	$550
Deed Prep	$100
Title Fee	$200
Total Closing	**$850**
Purchase + Rehab + Closing	$88,500

Sold $119,900 - $88,850 = $31,050 Profit

This deal took around 90 days to complete, the rehab only took around a week and then took around 80 days find a buyer and for the buyer to close on the property.

Rental Property Case Study

Here is an example of a purchase my father made.   He found a land lord who was looking to retire and just wanted to get out of his old rentals.   The land lord had 7 rentals he wanted to liquidate.   My Father negotiated with the land lord and got all 7 of the houses for $105,000, with the owner financing them.

$15,000 down, with a monthly payment of $950/month for 12 years.

Houses	Monthly Rent
#1	$485
#2	$425
#3	$525
#4	$450
#5	$475
#6	$550
#7	$475
Total	**$3,385**

Payment	$950
Taxes & Ins	$350
Total	**$1300**

$2,085/ Month in Cash Flow

The Tenants are Rapidly Paying off all of these homes. There are some repair costs associated with these houses. Tenants moving out but when you have good help and screen your tenant's right, you do not have to worry about your tenants trashing your place. It does happen though, so always have some cash saved up so you can make the repairs.

An Example of Adding Value to a Property

Purchased this property for $40,000, owner financed 4% for 10 years, $2,000 down payment; the payment is $332/month.

The House was a 3 bed 1 bath home around 1500 sq ft.

It also had a 750 sq ft building in the back which was used as a taxidermy shop at one time. The shop was insulated and had a bathroom.

We remodeled the 3 bed room house; it was flee infested and needed paint, carpet, appliances and minor work.

Then we remodeled the 750 sq ft building and turned it into a 2 bed 1 bath house. We expanded the bathroom and added a kitchen.

The total rehab cost for these two houses was around $10,000.

The 3 bed room house rents for $550 a month and the converted house rents for $500 a month.

That's a $1050 gross monthly rent.

Expenses: Payment = $332/month

Tax and Insurance = $100 $432 total monthly Expenses

That comes to $618/ month net cash flow.

The property also came with an additional lot which we can build on in the future. The property is also zoned commercial.   If you will note from the pictures, you could see a broken window in the back. It's a good thing I drove by and took the pictures and the tenants will be getting a phone call first thing Monday morning.

Chapter 10

Flipping Mobile Homes

I know you might be thinking I don't want to fix up Mobile Homes. I do not want to deal with the people who live in mobile homes and mobile homes always seem to have problems. Well, I am here to tell you that Mobile homes can be one of the best ways to start as a new investor or even an experienced investor like my father who got started flipping and renting mobile homes around 10 years ago, had wished he would have started sooner.

With the current state of the economy right now, there are thousands of people looking for affordable homes. Some of these people may have been foreclosed on and now cannot qualify to buy a regular home. Mobile homes offer them a great option. I will give you a few examples of Mobile home flips that my father and I had done.

The Key to mobile home flipping is to find motivated mobile home sellers, much like investing in single family Homes. There are several options you can do with these mobiles,

- You can fix them up and re-sell them for cash
- Fix them up and sell with owner financing
- You can rent them out.

I have done all of the above options and all are great.

- You get monthly payments
- No calls to unclog the toilet at 2 a.m. because they own the mobile
- You make more with interest

What I think is amazing, is that mobile homes take way less time to get sold. I have put up one craigslist ad for a mobile home and received 30 or more calls and emails from people looking to buy.

You can pick up mobile homes for under $10,000, rent these homes for $500 a month or more and make $6,000 in rent for the year. After deducting your expenses, you could still come out with a 40 - 50% return on your Money.

It does not take long to become very wealthy by earning 50% on your money.

Example 1:

410 Ed Street

Purchased for $3,500

Repairs $500

Total Investment $4,000

Resold for $7,500 $1,000 Down Payment 12% Interest for 3 years $6,500x 12% = $215.89

215.89 x 12 = $2,590.72 / $3,000 ($4,000-$1,000 Down Payment) = 86% return on your Money.

If you found 10 mobiles to do the above example with, you could create a $2,158.90/month income. All you would need is $30,000 in cash. You could borrow that money or use a private money lender.

Example 2: Rental Income Mobile Home

Purchased a 14x 70 2 Bed 1 Bath Mobile

Purchased price of $4,000

Repairs of $500

Total Investment $4,500

Rented to a Section 8 tenant (government pays their rent every month, guaranteed rent)

Rented for $500 a month, Lot rent is $140/per month, Taxes and Insurance $25/month

$500 - $140 - $25 = $335/ month cash flow

$335 x 12 = $4020/year $4020/ $4500 = 89% return on your Money.

The best part is after the14th month; you will have your total investment back and have cash every month coming in. Are you starting to see how a little mobile home can bring you huge returns with little money?

Example 3: Cash Mobile Home Flip 3 Bed Room 2 Bath

Purchased for $4,500
Repairs of $1,824.57
1 Month Lot Rent $295
Total Investment $6,619.57

Sold to someone looking to live in the mobile home for $15,000

$15,000 - $6,619.57 = **$8,380.43**

This deal took around 3 weeks totally to fix up but then took another month to close on it; the buyer was trying to sell another property he had and was waiting for title glitches to be cleared.

I did most of the work myself, I worked a few hours a day for a couple of weeks and hired a handy man to do a little of the work.   The only thing I did on the outside of the trailer was to seal the roof. This deal was actually done in November 2010.

Below are a few pictures of before and after. This is one of the very few before and after pictures that I have taken because while doing the project, I started to write this book and thought it would be a good thing to have.

My Final Thoughts on mobile homes.

I want you to change your beliefs on mobile homes. As you can see from the examples above they can produce amazing cash flow and can easily create financial freedom for anyone.

I highly suggest you start looking for mobile homes when you are out and about looking for houses. Start posting bandit signs around mobile home parks, and start posting ads saying I buy Mobile homes. Get out and make it happen.

Chapter 10

All Deals Are Not Created Equally

What to do when S#!% hits the Fan

"Do you know the difference between education and experience? Education is when you read the fine print; experience is what you get when you don't."

-Pete Seeger

So you might be thinking, "Wow, all this sounds so simple" and you're right, the process is pretty simple. There will be times when problems come up. I want to address some of the common problems that I have come across when buying real estate. There are several different things that can kill your deal or just postpone it for a while.

Wholesaling: Cannot Find a Buyer for your Cheap Property

Ok, so you have what you think is a killer deal; you have run the numbers, put your property under contract and started marketing the property like a mad man but no one seems to be interested in your property.   This will happen.

 You can either cancel the contract and walk away or go back to the seller and try to get the property at a lower price.

Do not get frustrated. Deals fall apart all the time because of financing, inspection or the buyer's mother did not like the house (this actually happened to a realtor friend of mine).   The point is that deals fall apart. As long as you took a few steps to protect yourself, there will be no problem.

You might be asking yourself right now, "If I cancel the deal, won't I lose my deposit?"

I know for a fact that you want to know how to never lose a deposit again, right?

One of the biggest fears in real estate is losing money, I know because I have that fear too. No one likes to lose money. There are steps or precautions you can take to make sure you always get your deposit back.

First off I want to talk about the amount of the deposit you are giving. What is a normal deposit you should give?

Some people will say $500, some will say $1000 and some will say it depends on how much the property is worth. Now I don't have a real good answer for this but I say it depends on how much competition you have. If there is 0 competition try and give as little as possible. I know a real estate investor who gives a $10 deposit on all of his contracts, yes $10 and he told me not one seller has ever cared.

That is kind of a way to never lose a deposit; I know that all of us can afford to lose $10. Try it out and just have confidence. Tell them that you always give $10 and that the deposit does not really mean much.

Now if there are tons of completions I would give whatever you can. If you know it's a smoking deal, give $5,000 if you have to. Sometimes when there is lots of competition, you have to give a big deposit to show the seller that you are ready to buy now.

Make sure that the Deposit is kept at the <u>title company</u> and that you never give the deposit to the seller. Always tell them that the deposit will be held in escrow at the title company. You think you will get your $500 deposit back from a seller who is in foreclosure? No way. They will keep it and run. We typically put up a $100 deposit when purchasing from an individual seller and $500 when the house is listed by a realtor.

Inspection Period

Every time you get a property under contract you should have some sort of inspection period, usually between 7 and 20 days. Anytime from the time you sign the contract until the time the inspection period runs out you can cancel the contract because the property did not pass your inspection. How great is that?

All you have to do is simply mail the seller a letter referring to section whatever of the contract the property does not pass our inspection and we are canceling the contract. Or you could go back and try to negotiate a lower price.

If you Notice in the First 10 days you can't sell the property, get out. You can always find something wrong, believe me. A better deal will come along, just be patient.

Partners Approval

In all of my contracts, I always make the contract contingent upon partner's approval. This serves a few good reasons. For one, sometimes I do not have the time to run a deal by my partner. I get a call and go to a property and sign a contract.

If I have over looked a few small details, I could have made a mistake and put property that just sucks under contract. Sometimes we get too focused on just putting deals together. My partner will then look the deal all over again and will sometimes say; hey this deal is just not for us.

With a contingency in my contract that says I can cancel if my partner does not approve, then I can just get out.

It also gives you another loop hole. Because sometimes a house will be in great shape and an inspection will not really reveal any major damages and if you say to the home owners *"ya, this house does not pass my inspection"* they will want to know why? What was wrong?

You can instead simply say *"my partner does not approve of this deal, we need to be at a lower price for him to approve"*. That way you can either get the property for a lower price or just get out of the deal.

Doing Your Homework

Another way to never lose a deposit is to really do your homework. What do I mean? I mean evaluate the deal thoroughly and make sure the deal is going to work.

The best way to know if a deal is going to work is to know what your wholesale buyers want in a deal. Then when you find a deal that meets their criteria, they will buy it right away.

Knowing that they want a 3 bed 2 baths is not enough. You have to know what their price range is, what part of town they want to invest in and how much they will pay. I have found that most investors will tell you oh I will look at any deal.

Tell them no that's not how I work. I only work with a selected few buyers and I have to know their specifics or I do not work with them.

Sit down with them, get out a sheet of paper and make 3 columns. "Must have", "Don't want" and "Maybe". Ask them to answer all of the questions. Also, ask them what is the highest amount they will pay for a house in a certain area and why? Asking why gives you a better understanding about the properties you are looking for.

Back to Deal Killers

Ok, I may have got off topic for a little bit there, but I had remembered something important. Let's get back to talking about things that may kill your deal.

The Title Will Not Clear

If you do several deals, you will come across this problem. As I am writing this, I am going through this problem with a rehab project. The title not clearing and has delayed our deal for around a month. There is nothing we could do about this. When the buyer bought the property, he filed things wrongly and didn't fill out the right documents and it's just been a mess. However, we are hanging in there and hoping to close soon. We are buying the deal at $20,000 and it needs $10,000 in work so we are hoping to sell it for $75- $85,000. Not too bad. So hang in there when there is a nice profit to be made.

If you are just beginning in real estate and do not know, every house has a Title. These titles have to be filed with the state in order to be eligible for title insurance (which we always get), and they need to be filed properly.

If someone who has owned the house filed the deed improperly the title company will be required to track that person down and get them to sign a quit claim deed. Or you will need to get approval from a judge after giving them your case.

A lot of times your current seller will have to go to court and file for a "quiet title". This is just a way to make sure the title does not cause you problems.

There is really nothing that can be done, just leave it up to your attorney and title company to get everything figured out. You will want to sign a new contract with the seller extending the contract date to when the title clears.

Do not get discouraged, just let the process work itself out and if you just do not want to deal with this, cancel the contract and move on.

If you have ever bought a house, you may be a believer of good and bad Karma. I have walked through a few houses and just had a bad feeling about them, maybe the layout was weird or the house was just creepy.

Below is a deal that I had put under contract but after a few days I just had a bad feeling and canceled my contract.

I had the property under contract for 50% of the ARV but still, it was just a bad deal. Not only did the property need lots of work, it also had a funky layout, weirdo seller, small lot and bad karma.

Use your judgment, not all houses that need lots of work are bad deals.

Seller just Disappears

This has happened a few times to me and has happened several times to my Partner. You think you have a great thing going, you are negotiating and are getting ready to put a property under contract, the seller seems happy.

But then you cannot find the seller, no answer on his phone, his house is now vacant and he has skipped town.

Believe me when I tell you this can be frustrating. I was going to try to do a short sale for a guy, the house was in a good location, nice lay out and needed zero work. I had talked with him about it, and he was excited. He just wanted to get rid of the house; he had already moved to a different state and bought a new house.

So I got all the paper work together and sent it to him. He said that he received it and would get it back to me. A few days went by and no calls. I called several times and no answer. The guy just disappeared.

After a few months I saw the house had went to foreclosure. You cannot help people who do not want to get help.

Someone Else Steals your Deal

There are dishonest real estate investors out there. Yes, it's true that some people just do not care and will go behind your back to get a deal, even if you have a property under contract. I have not had this happen to me yet but have talked to the president of my REIA and she has had a few people who had done this.

You can protect yourself by always getting the property under contract first and then filing the contract with your city's clerk and recorder. This puts a cloud on the title and if the dishonest buyer tries to get title insurance, the title company will see that you have had a contract in place first.

If this happens do not worry, there are hundreds of deals out there.

Well that wraps up some of the common reasons a deal may go bad. I know there are other reasons that will come up and every situation is different. Just be on the lookout and just keep moving forward.

Bonus Section

How to Build Multiple Streams of Income

"I would rather earn 1% off a 100 people's efforts than 100% of my own efforts"

-John D. Rockefeller

If you're like me, you would want to make as much money as possible and become financially free. Is that correct? To become financially free you have to always have cash flow coming in from several different sources.

Your Cash Flow can come in many different forms. Cash Flow from having Tons of Wholesale deals in the pipeline, rental properties, or other income streams.

Being a real estate investor you have several different things you can do to generate extra income.

As a real estate investor you generate leads of people who want to sell a house. So how can you use the leads to make extra income?

Every lead that comes in is not going to be a deal for you. Some people just want too much for their house, some owe too much, or some you just don't want to deal with.

Realtors

What do you do with a lead, where the seller wants too much for their house? You could refer them to a realtor and get a referral fee from that realtor.   Now to get a referral fee from a realtor you have to be a licensed realtor yourself. But if you're not licensed there is a trick you can do.

You can have the realtor buy some marketing campaigns for you. Have the realtor put your money in a fund and then once a referral commission comes in, have him buy some sort of marketing campaign for you. You could do commercials, bus benches, billboard or whatever you want.

Short Sale Investors

If you are doing lots of marketing you will be contacted by a few or hundreds of people who owe more than their house is worth.   You cannot wholesale a house that has no equity. So what you can do is refer them to a short sale investor. If short sales are your niche then you can do them yourself.

 Me personally I don't like short sales and would rather just refer them out and get a commission later.   Just make sure you have something in writing with your short sale investor that says you will get X amount of dollars for every lead or a certain % of the deal.

Sell Them to Other Investors

Ok, I know what you're saying, "Sell Them to Other Investors? Why Don't I just wholesale them". There are some deals that I come across that seems like it could be a good deal but I just have a bad feeling about it. I just don't even want to deal with the situation or seller. So what you can do is just be a bird dog and refer another investor to them.

Coach someone

Another way to bring in some extra income is to coach or mentor some other investors in your area. I know there are always new investors who want to get started but have no idea how. I would bet that several would pay a pretty penny for you to show them. Or Even Partner with them on wholesale deals. You could have the student do all the marketing, and then you just help them with the fine details and hold their hands and make 40 or 50% of their deal.

You could also teach your students to become property scouts for you. These scouts can find you a lot more deals.

Affiliate Marketing

The last source I am going to talk about is selling real estate investing materials, products and books to other investors. If you're a big time investor, you should already have a buyers list. These are people who are interested in real estate investing right? Of course they are.   So start telling them about cool products you that find.

Most big time real estate investing courses let you become an affiliate and sell their products. You get around 50% of the price of the product.   I use my Blog and email list to sell other investors products and I have been making a few thousands a month doing this.   I love having a few thousand dollars extra a month.

You are going to be setting up a Blog for internet marketing so why not make some money from it.

You can join my Affiliate Program and Make money by selling my **"Real Estate Flipping Secrets eBook"** I am giving affiliates 50% commission right now. So if someone buys this eBook through you, you get paid.   Sign up by going to.

http://realestateflippingriches.com/affiliates

You may also want to learn about affiliate marketing. I have read tons of eBooks on the topic and am still learning.

If you would like to get a list of some affiliate marketing courses, I recommend that you contact me.

It's Your Time for Success

"Obstacles are the things you see when you take your eyes off the goal"

The time is now to start creating your future. You have a few choices right now.

1. You can choose to do nothing
2. You can go at this half assed and most likely quit in month
3. You can apply what you have learned to change your life.

Which choice do you like? I hope that you choose number 3. I know that you can do this and become successful. It's going to take work, dedication and sacrifice.

If you do not start now you may never start. There is never going to be an ideal time to start creating your future. Another excuse will always come up, I want you to ignore all of your excuses and act today.

Right now there is so much opportunity out there. Houses are selling at an all-time low; investors are looking like crazy for cheap houses.

I recommend everyone start out by wholesaling. Just imagine if you only did one wholesale deal a month that brought you in $8,000, that's $96,000 a year and it's not hard to find one deal a month.

Step 1: Find Motivated Sellers

Try several different ways to market your business and find motivated sellers.

- Network
- Mailers
- Bandit Signs
- Classified Ad's

Step 2: Make Offers

Remember if you are not making offers you are not making money.

Step 3: Build Your Buyers List

A successful Wholesaler has a big list of buyers. (but remember all you really need is 1 great buyer)

Step 4: Make Money

It's all about creating a future for yourself and your family. Plus Making

Step 5: Have Fun!

Super Special Bonus

HOW to Work Less Yet Make More Money!

The big picture behind real estate investing is to give you freedom. We all want the freedom to do what we want and when we want to. Real Estate investing is one of the best vehicles to help you achieve these goals. This is why working smart and not harder is a huge key in building your real estate investing business. You want to create a business that will pretty much run on auto pilot and send you checks.

It's going to take some time to get to that point but there are hundreds of things you can outsource today to save yourself hundreds of hours.

In this section I am going to help you create a road map to outsourcing. Every business is different which means you will be outsourcing different tasks.

What are the tasks in your business you should outsource?

Think of the repetitive, tedious, and/or unimportant tasks in a real estate investing business that someone making minimum wage could easily master. These are the task that you need to know how to do but can easily outsource. One way to look at it is to look at what tasks are necessary in your business but require the least amount of specialized skill to complete. The first thing that I usually start to outsource is marketing tasks.

Things like writing and sending mailers, posting classified ads, contacting sellers online.

Here is a simple formula that you can use to start outsourcing your business.

Step 1: Compile a list of everything you do in your business.

Thing about everything that goes on in your business, marketing, mailers, calling sellers, posting property for sale, contacting craigslist ads, etc. Think about everything someone else could do.

Step 2: Pick 3 to 5 takes you want to outsource first

I suggest you pick a few of the jobs/tasks that you simple do not like doing. For example in my business we hand address all of my envelopes and stuff all of my mailers. I really did not like doing this so I hired someone to do this for me.

Here are a Few Things I suggest you Outsource

Marketing for Deals

- Pulling Foreclosure Files online and putting them into excel format so you can easily mail them out.
- Posting classified ads online.
- Emailing online Classified Ads

- Finding Deals on the MLS
- Putting our Bandit Signs (person in your town)
- Posing articles online
- Stuffing, stamping, addressing and mailing your yellow letters. (person in your town)

Talking to Sellers and Analyzing deals
- Calling Back Sellers and going over the lead sheet with them
- Evaluating deals and making initial offers to sellers
  - Have them make 5 to 10 offers a day.

Marketing for Cash Buyers
- Posting classified ads
- Posting wholesale property for sale online
- Using freedomsoft to contact and update buyer info.

This is just a few things you can have your assistant/ virtual assistant do. Create your business however you want to run it.

Recommended sites for hiring VA's

Odesk.com
Odesk is a site where you can post a job and have hundreds of qualified applicants contacting you. I have used odesk several times and find it to be one of the easiest to use sites. You can track your VA's work progress and see exactly how many hours the VA is

Billing you for. You can also easily make payments to them via odesk.

Craigslist.org
Everyone knows craigslist. Craigslist is one of the best sights to find motivated workers. Just post a job and you will have several people contracting you.

Elance.com
This is another place where VA's post their resumes.   You can find someone that can do just about anything on elance.

Posting your AD

Below is an example ad

Headline:
Wanted! Awesome Real Estate Investing VA.

Body:
I'm Looking for a full time VA to help with marketing my Real Estate Business Online.

Responsibilities Include
-Daily Posting on Craigslist --- up to 5 ads per day
and other online classified ad sites.
-Responding to Motivated Seller Listing on Craigslist
-Posting real estate property listings on Blogs and Craigslist
-Writing and re-writing articles

-Posting articles and videos on my word press Blogs -20
-Sorting Microsoft excel data

***Must ***
Speak English
Know how to post on word press
Know how to post on craigslist
Microsoft Word and Excel knowledge
Google Documents

Once I start getting applicants I usually weed out all of the people who have ZERO experience (it will show on their profile) and also anyone that has bid the job over $4. When hiring a VA I want to pay less than $3 per hour. But that is just me, pay whatever you feel comfortable paying.

The second thing I do is send an email to everyone that has applied and looks like a good candidate that says simply " Hi this is Christopher Seder and I want to thank you for applying, we will make a hiring decision very soon, I have a couple quick questions for you. What rate do you bill at and when can you start. Thanks"
I send this message first to see how fast they respond back to me. I want a VA that is going to respond back within an hour. If the applicant takes more than 2 hours to respond back, he/she is then taken out of the applicant pool.

Once you have narrowed it down to a few applicants you should set up a few phone or skype interviews. Always trust your instincts when hiring a VA.

The Number one Secret to Creating an Awesome VA

Training and giving your VA a clear vision on what they are to be doing is the number one way to have success with a VA. If you just tell them do go do this and not explain to them or have a clear step by step guide to follow then your VA will be running around with his head cut off.

I personally like to create Step by Step easy to follow screen shot videos for my VA's to follow. Go out and create videos or guides on every repeatable/ easy process in your business.

So there you go. I am completely confident that I have given you enough information to go out and hire a VA for your business. Remember to always trust your own judgment when hiring a VA and take your time when hiring. You may have to sort through a few bad VA's to find that perfect fit for your business but he/she is out there.

Real Estate Coaching

Most people I know that are successful in real estate investing are successful because they have a mentor to show them the way. I would not be successful if I did not have my father a 30 year real estate veteran who is always around to answer any of my questions and get me going.

"One of the chief reasons for Dell's remarkable run from start-up to worldwide leader in market share, said Fortune magazine in 2005, is that 'Michael Dell surrounded himself with mentors and consultants when he needed to'."

- Kate Ludeman, author of Alpha Male Syndrome

"Our greatest weakness lies in giving up. The most certain way to succeed is always to try just one more time."

- Thomas Edison

"'Come to the edge,' He said. They said, 'We are afraid.' 'Come to the edge,' He said. They came. He pushed them...and they flew."

- Guillaume Apollinaire

Perhaps you have asked yourself this question before: "Self, why do I not have vast mountains of hot, sweaty, sexy cash?"

No doubt yourself answered you back with something to this effect, "because you're just not lucky" or "because that's for other people – not you" or "because your parents were poor" [so were mine] or even better… "because you're ugly."

Thanks a lot, *Self*. We are our worst enemy and if we are to have any success whatsoever, we must begin telling ourselves who's boss in this land.

The first thing we can do to reclaim our lives for the true champion selves is that we really need to start asking better questions. We might better ask, "Self, how can I *get* vast mountains of hot, sweaty, sexy cash?" See the difference?

The former focuses on the negative and the latter on the positive. Whatever you ask yourself … you will get the answer. Start asking yourself every day, "What can I do to become the smashing success that I know I was born to be?"

So long as when you ask this you have tapped into the true subconscious "you" who will never lie to you but will always guide you along the correct and most prosperous path, you should hear something back along these lines …

"Hire Christopher Seder as your personal real estate investment mentor. Do it now. Go. Right now. Do it."

Now let's not kid ourselves friends; there are times when you should NOT follow your heart. It will get you into all types of trouble on occasions. Luckily for you and I … This is not one of those times. You need to listen to the True You on this one and **get on the path that leads to the mountain.** That's right – The Mountain of Hot, Sweaty, *Sexy* Cash.

I'm already playing on this mountain. So are my friends. It's a fun mountain; believe me. It's better here. We all run around with wheelbarrows full of the stinky cash and toss it around. We make big salads out of it and eat it for lunch. Heck, we even roll around in it and make money angels just like how we used to do in the snow when we were kids. It's awesome.

We burn cash for the fun of it here. It's hot. It's sweaty. And it's sexy. What more do you want?

> *"A good coach will make his players see what they can become rather than what they are."*
>
> ### - Ara Parseghian

SUCCESS KEY

**You will seldom improve your situation
if you have no one to copy but yourself!
Why?
Because your*self … Is an idiot!***

The TRUE Secret To My Success

I attribute probably 80% of my success to MY original mentor in real estate whose biggest service to me was showing me what is truly possible. I would've never thought what I'm doing was possible had I not personally witnessed it in his life with my own two eyeballs.

He does the same exact thing I will be teaching you to do and he is on track to make millions this year and own over 100 rentals. He has No employees and spends zero dollars per year on marketing. Did I mention he has been **flipping houses for over 30 years** and been involved in over **1200 real estate transactions?** Yeah. True story.

You Wanna BE A Millionaire?

Start ASSOCIATING With Millionaires.

All my friends roll like this. They're all young millionaires or millionaire "minded" on their way to the top. You need to surround yourself with these types of people if you hope to experience success for yourself. "He who dwells with the wise will be wise" so goes the proverb. It could be restated with just as much truth as "He who dwells with the prosperous will be prosperous." This is a time proven principle; whoever you hang around – you will become.

Ever notice how you inevitably start picking up all the weird sayings, terminology, and antics as your best friend? Just happens almost automatically doesn't it? Hhmmm. I wonder if we pick up their bad habits and attitudes as *well*.. Interesting.

SUCCESS KEY

The More Successful People You Are Exposed To, The More Successful You Will Become!

Bottom line – Hang around losers who talk about how much the real estate market sucks and you will soon find yourself broker than a dork who sits around and talks about how much the real estate market sucks. Hang around me and MY friends … And you will soon find yourself flipping houses like flap jacks on a Saturday morning before cartoons and making what I like to call "SEXY CASHOLA". Sounds like a cereal that mixes cash in with granola for a sexy breakfast treat. Yum. I want seconds.

Team Freedom is making money no matter WHAT the market is doing!!!!!!!!!!

THE Big Sky Property Solutions LLC V.I.P. APPRENTICESHIP PROGRAM

What it is NOT:

Classes, seminars, workbooks, homework, weekly phone calls, etc …

What it IS:

A one-on-one apprenticeship/partnership with Yours Truly for 12 months. We are basically just doing business together.

You also get all of my courses that I have put together and ever will put together. (That's a bazillion dollar value)

Whats in it for you!

What you will learn: Everything. How to negotiate deals, what deals are good, what deals are bad, how to determine value, how to get things sold quickly, how to do things risk free, how to expedite closings, etc., etc.. How to BE THE BEST. By the end of 12 months you will know how to do what I do. All that I am will rub off on YOU.

How much time it takes on a weekly basis? As much as you have to put into it. I started myself part time while working another full time job and then went full time whenever I could afford to do so. I have other students who have done the same.

How much access you will have to me? Pretty much unlimited. Within reason. My experience has been that by offering unlimited access to me, you guys tend to not abuse it. You will have my private personal email that I check a billion times a day.

What work is involved on your part? At first the only thing you have to worry about is finding leads (motivated sellers). My book has plenty of information to get your started in this regard. Get creative. Everyone's preferred method of lead generation is different. Everything else you will learn as we go.

Finding leads, by the way, is the easy part. It's what to do with them that takes some learning.

Where will we get the money to buy houses? We will be assigning contracts which does not require any money. If a deposit is required, we will supply it. All financial obligations rest on my shoulders, not yours. Heck of a nice way to start eh?

Who is responsible for selling the properties? You are, under our guidance. I will assist you in building a buyer's list and with marketing locally in the most effective manner possible.

Who is responsible for escrow deposits on properties? I put up all deposits.

Where the closings will be? My title company.

The Investment:

$2,000 up front and we split profits 50-50 for as long as you want to continue sending leads to us (Minimum of 5 transactions). My fees are rising to $5,000 soon. In the future it might be at the higher price.

Let me ask you a question. How much do you honestly think another real estate coach is going to help you in your efforts to get your deals CLOSED (as in, "check in your bank account" **CLOSED**) when they have no interest in the deal? We are going to make DANG sure your deals close because YOUR deals are OUR deals!

As a side note, 50% of profits is darn generous. Bring a lead to any other wholesaler and they will give you $500. I will be giving you more like $5,000 to $20,000 per deal AND teaching you an industry in the process. I have a friend who spent $20,000 for his mentoring!

I accept all major credit cards. If you would like a payment plan, you can do **$297 up front and payments of $197 a month for 12 months**. That comes out to $2,661. So you will end up Saving $661 by paying upfront.

>>>>>>> __ChristopherSeder.com/Application__ <<<<<<

**Space is always limited in this program, and people who pay the whole amount up front (making things less complicated) get first priority.

Why I am doing this is in the first place? I mean, aren't I just creating competition for myself? I sure am. Ask me how much I care. Dude, there is so much business out there it just doesn't matter. And you need to think like that too or else your chances of succeeding are nil. I mean, I started out knowing NOTHING and I was finding deals making $20,000, $35,000, $50,000 on a flip not even knowing what I was doing hardly. There are more deals than there are investors. TRUST me. Plus …'m better than all of you. That will never change. :)

The REAL reason I'm doing this is simply out of the kindness of my heart. I'm donating all the money to charity.

SIKE!

I'm doing this to make you and me a lot of money in a win-win situation!! Duh. And in all actuality I do give a LOT to church and charity. How much? I'll give you a hint – 10% is for stingy people.

A while back a friend of mine from called me up and said he had heard about my success in real estate. He informed me that he had just spent a bazillion dollars on the **Rich Dad real estate coaching program** (never did one deal). He wondering if maybe I could do something better for him.

Well I sat down and started thinking about it and I asked myself if there was some way that I could do this while (A.) Making it worth my while and (B.) Offering value to him. The more I thought about it, the more I liked the idea. But I wanted to make sure that whatever

I charged for a fee I was offering back value times a hundred. I am 100% convinced that I have successfully met that goal. My service to my students is invaluable in my (and their) opinion. $2,000 is chump change compared to what you will get in return.

Here is what a typical transaction will look like for you:

- You get an incoming call from some of the super cheap marketing that I've instructed you to do.

- You will fill out a simple lead sheet that I have given you up front.

- You tell the prospect, "Great. I'll look into this and get back to you right away."

- You then email that lead sheet to me and I take it from there. How easy is that???

- I then look at the deal, tell you what makes it good or bad, tell you what we need to offer or why we need to pass on it, help you write up the contract, and literally walk you through every step of the deal until we have sold it and made at LEAST $10,000 (or as much as $50,000 or more) which we split at the time of closing.

- The title company will send or wire you your 50% of the deal directly

We do enough of these deals and you will have made a LOT of money and learned an industry in the meantime.

I look forward to working with you and being used by God to help you realize the success that you were put on earth to achieve.

To Your Success,

Christopher $eder

http://ChristopherSeder.com/application

THE END

p.s. **You need a coach**, and you know it. Ask any successful real estate investor or wholesaler if they had a mentor and they will ALL tell you "yes." Did you know that Jack Nicholas, the greatest golfer of all time STILL pays big money for a coach? What does that say to you? Stop trying to beat the world on your own. IT'S IMPOSSIBLE! I'm at the other end of the tunnel shining a light back at you, waving you over. Now get your butt over here. It's funner on the other end. We've got cookies.

p.p.s. – I love you.

p.p.p.s. – All successful people have one thing in common. *They act.* They are quick to act and slow to change that decision.

Look for these other Courses from Christopher Seder

Vacant House Riches

 In this course Christopher Seder shows you how to find and flip vacant houses. Vacant houses are his #1 way to find Killer Real Estate Deals.

Go to http://VacantHouseRiches.net for more info.

Christopher Seders $1 Action Plan

 This is a 30 day action plan designed to give you step by step guidance to finding and flipping your first deal. With this dollar action plan you will also get a 30 day free trail of Christopher Seders RealEstateVIPCoaching.com
To get your action plan go to

http://realestateflippingriches.com/action

Real Estate Flipping Riches
<u>FREE</u> Video Course

Inside this 7 steps to real estate riches, you'll discover How **ANY** one can start flipping houses today, have *fun*, and generate MASSIVE amounts of cash... and learn for FREE:

How to Get Started and Your First Flip

The Most Important Video You Will Ever Watch

Wholesaling – How to Flip Houses For Quick Cash

Fix and Flip Houses – How to Make Large Sums of Cash

The Art of Marketing – How to Find Thousands of Amazing Real Estate Deals

The Secrets of Rental Success

How to Create Other Sources of Income

http://RealEstateFlippingRiches.com

Sign Up Today For FREE